Praise for *Chingona*

"Whether you identify with the Latin heritage or not, *chingona* is a word that all free, autonomous, authentic, thinking, fiery women can identify with. Dr. Alma Zaragoza-Petty's recollection of her upbringing and how she has journeyed to reclaim the term is a sisterhood chat we all need to hear. The words in this book are the healing balm and permission we all need to reclaim the selves that we were told had to look or be a certain way in order to be seen, heard, or valued. Zaragoza-Petty reminds us that the chingona is worthy and deserves to be celebrated."

—**Arielle Estoria**, spoken word poet, actor, and speaker

"The more detached from our feelings and our body's visceral responses, the stronger and more celebrated we seem to be perceived. A kind of perverse admiration. *Chingona* is deeply honest and vulnerable. Liberating. There is a sense that Alma Zaragoza-Petty's journey centers the self in ways that many of us have needed to—yet not in a way that is self-absorbed nor destructively self-interested. She invites all of us to a self-centering that discovers and honors the stories of our histories; de nuestro antepasados; de Dios. What a badass testimonio!"

—**Rich Pérez**, author, speaker, and filmmaker

"*Chingona* is filled with lyrical storytelling and liberating truths. If you are looking for a book to challenge and empower you, this is the book to read. Grab a highlighter because you'll need it!"

—**Faitth Brooks**, author, speaker, and educator

"Don't look for warm fuzzy self-help in Alma Zaragoza-Petty's raw, honest, and powerful book. Personal development never looked so human and non-white male. Zaragoza-Petty offers a gift to monocultural readers: insight into the realities of twenty-first-century multicultural experience. For us multicultural readers, she holds up our liminality as sacred and a core part of justice-centering as she weaves between stories and language, pain and healing, unjust realities and hope."

—**Kathy Khang**, activist and author of *Raise Your Voice: Why We Stay Silent and How to Speak Up*

"In *Chingona*, la doctora offers a brave and rare testimonio of the Chicana/Latina experience. Incorporating the best of Chicanx Studies and critical race theory in education, she captures the struggle of so many of our sisters and primas and points us ultimately to Jesús, the prototype curandero."

—**Robert Chao Romero,** professor at University of California, Los Angeles, and author of *Brown Church: Five Centuries of Latina/o Social Justice, Theology, and Identity*

"*Chingona* is the book I wish I had growing up as a migrant Mexicana in the United States. Zaragoza-Petty writes from her heart and her mind, with poetic phrasing and beautiful attention to honoring her experience. She applies the concept of mija spirituality in a powerful way that invites her readers to heal, grow, and lead. I read *Chingona* with my mind and body. Some of the stories resonate so much with mine and, I imagine, with the stories of many Latinas and others who have experienced trauma. I am thankful that she has chosen her camino and invites us to do the same."

—**Noemi Vega**, speaker and coauthor of
*Hermanas: Deepening Our Identity and
Growing Our Influence*

"If you are a Black or brown woman that the world has tried to conquer, this book is for you. As an Afro-Latina, I find my own story in each page. I'm thankful that Alma Zaragoza-Petty was brave enough to show up as her whole self; it makes me feel visible. Bravo, Amiga!"

—**Ligia Noemi Cushman**, author, child welfare
consultant, and international speaker

"In *Chingona*, Dr. Alma Zaragoza-Petty brilliantly curates an enchanted world full of Indigenous wisdom and feminist charm. She offers us imagination for the future while showing us how to conquer every white supremacist narrative that so easily conquers all of us."

—**William Matthews**, singer-songwriter, artist, advocate, and former host of *The Liturgists* podcast

CHINGONA

CHINGONA

Owning Your Inner Badass for Healing and Justice

ALMA ZARAGOZA-PETTY

Broadleaf Books

Minneapolis

CHINGONA

Owning Your Inner Badass for Healing and Justice

Published in association with The Bindery Agency,
www.TheBinderyAgency.com.

Cover design: Mer Young

Print ISBN: 978-1-5064-8318-4
eBook ISBN: 978-1-5064-8319-1

CONTENTS

1

FOR BROWN WOMEN THE WORLD HAS TRIED TO CONQUER

In addition to the work of building the muscle of our imaginations, we must build the pathways by which we reach each other, make sure we can hear each other beyond the status quo.

—ADRIENNE MAREE BROWN

As a kid I spent hours in my local public library, reading fiction and nonfiction. My mother refused to check out books because of the fees I once incurred when I held on to a book for too long. So instead I went to the library, picked a comfortable seat, and escaped into books. The ideas those books offered helped me imagine different worlds and unseen possibilities. When I encountered new historical or scientific information or a concept I didn't understand, I turned to encyclopedias and dictionaries. (This was before the advent of the internet.) Some of the explanations left me confused and with more questions.

The women in my own family held stories and information and ways of knowing that were not at all like the narratives and concepts I was reading. Women like my grandmother and great-grandmother used their own knowledge and wisdom to cure anything from an empacho to a mal de amores. Learning from generations of Latina women and other women of color meant that, at home, I was hearing vastly different stories from the ones I encountered in books. Slowly over the years, I became aware of the legacy and heritage I had inherited—a legacy that those books, and the people who wrote them, denied me by their systematic erasure of the stories of my ancestors and foremothers. Those books helped me escape my own reality rather than enter more deeply into it.

Years later, as an adult, I would find books that helped me dive into the stories of women of color, including those in my own family. Only then would I find other Latina women, as well as Black and Indigenous women, who were reclaiming their lives through writing. Octavia Butler, Clarissa Pinkola Estés, Gloria Anzaldúa, bell hooks, Chrystos, Sandra Cisneros, Audre Lorde, Sara Ahmed—these and countless other feminists, revisionists, and visionaries inspired me. As brown women the rest of the world had been intent on conquering, they showed me another way of knowing.

As we get into what being a chingona means—what the word represents, how I came to own my chingona journey, and how you can too—I want to introduce you to my way of knowing and storytelling. Adrienne Maree Brown reminds us: "There is how we tell a story, and then there is the story we tell." It is important to start here because one of the reasons I wrote this book was that I did not see these narratives (the stories we tell) or these methodologies (how we tell them) represented in the books I read as a young girl. Like Brown, I am committed to "telling our own stories and generating new questions and problems that are relevant for currently marginalized peoples."

I am motivated to share my story because it is an old story, a story about healing ourselves and each other. It is a story still absent from so many books, and it is also a story we must never tire of telling, from all angles and positionalities. We must remind each other that hope is always possible and change is always accessible. For me, hope is about believing in each other and imagining a better world together, a world in which social justice and love flourish.

CHINGONA HISTORY

When I was growing up, a chingona was the last thing a good little Mexican girl wanted to be called. I didn't understand what the word meant; I just knew you didn't want to get called it. Like girls and women in many cultures, Latinas are often told a version of "calladita te vez mas bonita," or "you look prettier with your mouth shut." Not that I ever kept my mouth shut—ergo, why I was often called chingona. The fear of getting called chingona was used to keep good little Latina girls doing good little Latina girl things.

Chingona is a derogatory or vulgar term for a woman who is too aggressive or difficult or out of control. It has a masculine version, chingón—which is often used as a compliment. So when I was called a chingona, I knew it did not mean the same thing as when my male cousin was told *he* was a chingón. To be a chingón, at least in many circles, means you are the good kind of badass: a guy worthy of respect. To be a woman or girl, though, who is considered a chingona? Now that was a different story.

Although there is debate about the etymology of the word *chingar*, from which *chingona* and similar words derive, one thing is clear: it has violent, colonial, and patriarchal roots. The first people referred to as "hijos de la chingada" (literally translated "children of the fuck" or "sons of the raped woman") were the mestizo children born to Indigenous women who had been raped by Spanish colonizers.

The original chingada is sometimes considered to be La Malinche, a Nahua woman from the Gulf Coast and a prominent figure in

Mexican history. La Malinche was forced to work alongside the Spanish conquistador Hernán Cortés as a translator. She had been offered as a gift alongside other valuable objects—including other women—first to Mayan and then to Aztec leaders, before she was either sold or given to Cortés. She knew both Maya-Yucateca and Nahuatl, the two major languages in the region at that time. This made her a prized asset for the Spaniards. Due to La Malinche's key role in facilitating colonization, her life is well documented. She is credited with giving birth to Martín Cortés, who is considered to be one of the first mestizos, or people of mixed Indigenous and Spanish ancestry. La Malinche has thus come to be known as the mother of the "first mestizo." Her son, sometimes considered the first Mexican, was also the first "hijo de la chingada." The first chingón.

So being called a chingón or chingona still holds those colonial and patriarchal insinuations: that you are acting like a parentless—or more specifically a *fatherless*—child. It's like how "bastard" in English has come to refer to someone with no manners—someone who is difficult or improper. This is how mestizo children were seen by the Spaniards. To be called a chingona is to be considered an unclaimed person. A chingona is a brown woman who needs to be conquered—someone who is growing up to become an unruly woman.

To be called a chingona means your whole existence is being called into question, especially when your own father or mother says it to you. It feels like you are being disowned, that you are no longer considered a part of the family due to whatever disagreeable behavior you are exhibiting.

Although I did not know the historical and violent roots of the word as a child, I instinctively felt that the word *chingona* was meant to keep me and other girls and women in our place. It was intended to remind us that we might as well be disowned children, like the first mestizos.

When I first set out to write and publish this book, I was tired of feeling that way: disowned, unloved, like a real hija de la chingada. I was barely holding on. I had just come out of several tumultuous years of healing and growth. I was searching for meaning and purpose in a life that felt empty and inconsequential. I think we all search for meaning and purpose at different points in our lives. We try to understand our roles with ourselves and each other. For me, those painful years mostly brought confusion. I had been wrestling with existential questions: why I am here—and for what? I was feeling of little importance. In fact, I was feeling the same way that being called a chingona as a child made me feel.

I had recently finished my doctorate in education. (I like to joke that I have a doctorate in learning about learning.) And while I did earn a doctor of philosophy degree in education in part because I love to learn, I also felt like an unwelcome outsider in university halls. Playing by the rules of higher education and reimagining the ivory tower from within it were not options for me. I have a lot of respect for those who have made academia their life's work, especially those from subjectivities and experiences that had historically been kept from such institutions. But as I finished my studies, I experienced what Gloria Anzaldúa calls a nepantla space: an in-between territory, a borderland. *Nepantla* is a Nahuatl word for, in Anzaldúa's words, "the space between two bodies of water, the space between two worlds. It is a limited space, a space where you are not this or that but where you are changing." As she writes, I was "feeling torn between identities," and my in-between identities made it hard for me to stay within the confines of one single discipline. I wanted to be free to explore various fields, genres, and theories and to question them without having to worry about promotions and tenure. I wanted to use what Dolores Delgado Bernal calls "cultural intuition." And I wanted to give myself time to heal by drawing strength and wisdom from others and from the past—to be rebuilt and reborn from the pain of the past, which I'll describe in these pages. I longed for a safer environment, a space where I could be in community with other women.

I also wanted to rest, pause, and reflect. I craved a wisdom beyond books. I wanted to fully live and be. I knew I would not find this inside the halls of the academy; instead, I would need to use intuition as my guide. I just didn't know what that meant yet. Now I know that during those years, I was deeply depressed. I was hungry to live but unsure of what I would live for. I had not yet learned how to be compassionate with myself or to reconnect with the spiritual aspects of life, the wisdom from my antepasados. For brown women the world has intended to conquer, the emotional labor of healing often results in feeling soul-loss. Learning to stay grounded despite a tremendous feeling of being spiritually hungover—reeling from processing difficult feelings and thoughts—is demanding work.

Finding conocimiento—a wisdom beyond academic knowledge, one that centers mind/body/spirit awareness—turned out to be a big rebelde and wild move for me. Many of us from communities of mixed heritage—whose ancestors were Black and Indigenous—as well as those whose ancestors were systematically oppressed in all sorts of ways: we have a legacy of survival and resistance. As a woman of Indigenous, Black, and Spanish descent, I have had to hold the complexity that even as some of my ancestors were being oppressed by colonization, others were inciting the harm. Many of us embody this intergenerational trauma. Many of us hold both the persecutor and the persecuted, the colonizer and the colonized, within our DNA. I knew I could find deep spiritual freedom and knowledge alongside our community—I just had to figure out how.

During those days, I sometimes thought back to being a young girl and being called a chingona. I thought of all the times I was considered too loud, too aggressive, too emotional. And I began to wonder whether becoming a real chingona—a woman who represents strength, courage, and authenticity, who knows who she is, where she came from, and how to make life better for herself and others—was something to move toward, not away from. I began to understand chingona not in terms of the oppressed mestiza but in terms of the surviving Indigena and Afrodescendiente. By owning my inner chingona, I could preserve my non-Spanish roots. What if La Malinche and the women who had raised me knew something I had yet to learn?

I needed to own my inner chingona rather than run away from her.

HOW WE RECLAIM CHINGONA

I'm not the first to reclaim this word, which has so often been used against Latina women. Over the last few years, many Chicanas and Latinas, abroad and in the United States, have begun using what was an insulting word as a badge of honor. We are repurposing chingona to mean "a real badass woman" in a good way, and we are using it to uplift one another as women. Nowadays, in many contexts, being called a chingona offers a sense of pride and dignity. It means you are admirable for your strength, general badassery, and overall perseverance in life despite systematic oppression and cultural erasure. "I wanted to find a positive way to say 'a woman who is on her path and who is powerful and is not being defined by a man but is being defined as a woman on her own path, on her direction, on her own intuitive powers,'" novelist Sandra Cisneros says about using the word *chingona* to describe herself. "I was trying to find a way to place a woman in her place of power when she's following her camino."

From social justice advocates to social media influencers, Latinas are redefining the word for ourselves and our communities. The word has gained popularity in pop culture, and artists and entrepreneurs are beginning to claim the term and put it in songs and poems and on products to sell. To some, it has already become overused, and yet to others, this term is still unknown. No matter how you understand it, the word is commonplace in the Latina community, and I'm glad that *chingona* has come to mean so much more than what it meant when I was girl.

I do not, by any means, claim to have a proverbial corner on the knowledge of what it is to be a chingona. I cannot tell you what it should mean to you; no one really can. We don't get rid of colonial legacies by reclaiming a single word that was used against us. What I do know is that no other word—in either English or Spanish—quite captures my experience the way that *chingona* does.

In the words of Angela Aguirre, "What truly defines us as chingonas is our ability to harness our fire." Embracing your chingonaness means you are an agent of change. When you own your inner chingona, you are confronting your pain and repurposing your experiences to heal yourself and those around you, including those who came before you and those who are yet to come.

Owning your inner chingona is an exercise of both intergenerational spiritual redemption and visionary leadership. Reclaiming your roots in a long lineage of badassery is not a new idea; it is embedded deeply in many of us who are survivors. I think of my own family members, mis tias and abuelas, who have fought incessantly for survival against toxic patriarchal relationships and capitalistic abuse of their service as cleaners, seamstresses, and caretakers. They were the first chingonas to teach me that change is possible and learn how to practice hope. I think of generations of Latina revolutionaries, the nameless women who fed, clothed, and took care of social justice movements to change laws that, by definition, did not consider their existence.

I think, too, of Tonantzin, the divine mother of the Mexicas and Nahua people, who reinvented herself as the Virgin Mary and appeared to Juan Diego Cuauhtlatoatzin, a Chichimec peasant, in the sixteenth century. In doing so, Tonantzin, who some know as Our Lady of Guadalupe, brought hope and faith amid forced religion conversion. She still inspires Indigenous people to claim hope in the middle of occupation and conquest. For many, Tonantzin and the Virgin of Guadalupe are one and the same. Just like La Malinche and Tonantzin, chingonas survive unspeakable harm and live to tell about it. They become nepantleras: boundary-crossers, border-dwellers.

Just like our foremothers, who bore the weight of colonialism and patriarchy and racism and survived, we, too, are forging our own path given the circumstances we have been born into. Future generations will come to see us as their ancestors. We are dreaming up new lives.

You could call this book a "big-ass testimonio." In addition to being a scholar and an activist, I am a daughter, a sister, a mother, a wife, and a friend. This book includes glimpses of all these roles. It is what theorists Daniel G. Solorzano and Tara J. Yosso call a "counterstory" to dominant narratives that otherize or discredit our lived experiences. Testimonio is a tool used in critical race theory to put a face to marginalized voices— those who are nearest to injustice. Giving testimonios is also the spiritual practice of narrating your story from a hope-filled and divine perspective in faith spaces. Academics might call this an autoethnography, but I call it a big-ass testimonio. The narratives in this book encompass all I've mentioned and are also a form of resilience and resistance. Owning your inner chingona is about telling a counterstory, offering a testimonio. Speaking or writing your story in your own way becomes a form of resistance.

Instead of being linear in my method of storytelling, I often let dreams, platicas, visions, and memories lead the way. For me, writing down my dreams and visions and memories has led the way to discovering the healing and growth milestones I could not see when I was muddled in the pain. It is leaning into my own intuition. In this way, the process of drafting this book was a highly spiritual one for me, and I hope the process of reading it is a highly spiritual one for you.

YOUR CHINGONA JOURNEY

To be a chingona means to be authentic—to live in your own way—and this book will help you on your journey of authentic healing and growth and leadership. Owning your inner chingona is a lifelong process with yourself and with those around you, past, present, and future. As we challenge ourselves to heal mind, body, and soul, we encourage those around us and thus transform our world. We develop a keen sense of pride in our ancestors, and we become peacemakers for future generations.

This spiritual awakening—because what else could it be called but that?—has eternal effects. Change is necessary for each of us, because we are all a part of a larger community. As we heal, we learn to acknowledge how much we need each other. Our confianza in each other begins to take root and increases as we own our inner chingona. We learn to trust each other. We *need* to trust each other, because that is part of why we are here: to love one another. As we heal individually from an often violent collective history, our spiritual and social awareness grows, and we embark on owning our inner chingona.

And I hope you know you are already a chingona, no matter where you are on your journey. I like to imagine the chingona process as always arriving but never having arrived. You restart, over and over again and throughout your life, and you move into your next chingona level. I hope this book helps you own your inner chingona. I hope that it reminds you of the ancestral wisdom and courage we carry. Since the birth of the first hijas de la chingada, women born of conquest have known more about survival and hope and justice than others may think.

I also hope that if you have already claimed your inner chingona, you are leading others into doing the same. We need more chingonas: idealists who want justice and healing and a different future from the history we inherited.

I hope this book takes you on a spiritual journey to becoming and embracing your whole self—including the parts of yourself that others may have mislabeled or misunderstood. I have often been given labels—like the term *chingona*—which have been used against me. The term *at-risk*, for example, which teachers and social workers often use to describe young chingonas like me, always felt like a word meant to put me and others like me in our place.

It takes a lot of strength to live a life beyond the labels and boxes others have put us in—and, just as important, the boxes and labels we continue to put *ourselves* in. Reclaiming not just the terms themselves but all of who we are is demanding work. Being a chingona means moving away from a place of fake security and safety that labels and boxes are meant to provide and moving toward authenticity. We find courage and purpose by living outside those self- and other-limiting beliefs.

Hopefully it has already become clear that norms and rules do not define chingonas. In my chingona journey, I refuse to believe, for example, that I cannot embrace a life of spirituality and social justice. In my chingona journey, I refuse to just pray harder, practice being happier, or think that things will change without effort, sacrifice, and dedication. I refuse to believe that we can only experience true healing in death, in some metaphysical space called heaven.

Instead, I have sought out therapy and authentic community, and I have reimagined spiritual practices, some of which I share in this book. And, yes, I took some meds. I desired to be healed in this lifetime and to be a force of change for my family. So I committed to breaking cycles of intergenerational trauma with the help of la virgencita, Jesús, and antidepressants. After many years of living with unresolved trauma, I finally confronted it all. And I was *absolutely* living in chingona territory.

As I advanced in my professional journey, I also did not accept that being a leader meant engaging in oppressive practices. Being a chingona meant finding another way to be a leader— not buying into models of success and leadership dependent on hurting or exploiting others. Even if it meant taking a longer, more tenuous, less desirable route, it was worth it. I am perfectly imperfect, and I have had to learn and relearn how to speak and act more inclusively. I am an educated, cisgender woman of color from a working-class background. As such, I occupy various privileged and nonprivileged intersections. I try to be continually aware of the power I do hold so that I can wield it well. But before abusing and misusing power was something I was even concerned with, I was simply trying to convince myself that my childhood wounds, and what I had labeled "failure," did not discredit me from leading. I was mending my own definition of what it means to be a leader, and I was learning to believe that I was a leader in my own right.

The world can only be as just as our "selves" are healed. Systemic change can only come from a place of healing within our own fractured selves. Having an inner world at peace is necessary to create a more just and peaceful society. The world is broken, and we are products of that world, so we need to heal and mend ourselves before assuming we can heal and mend the world and those around us. I am not saying we are inherently broken, but we are a part of broken systems meant to privilege some and oppress others. And if we are all living and leading from that brokenness, we will continue to contribute only brokenness to the world.

If you are Latina, you might already be aware of what it means to be a chingona in a general pop-culture sense of the word. But you get to define what it means to own your inner chingona. If you are here to just learn from an experience other than your own, welcome. Anyone, not just Latinas or women, can be chingonas. Nonbinary, femme identifying, and queer folks are some of the baddest chingonas; they've had to be. And if you aren't Latina, I simply ask that you enter my dream-filled, bilingual storytelling realm with respect and empathy. I do not italicize words from my language, because to do so would only contribute to otherizing myself, my community, and our experiences. So if you have never been confused by words, storytelling methods, or perspectives you don't understand in books, I ask you to simply sit in that discomfort as you read this book. So many of us have had to experience that discomfort for so long. Even so, learning to own your inner chingona might mean discovering we have more in common than you think. I hope my story is one that inspires you, no matter who you are or where you come from, to grow, heal, and lead others.

If you have already embarked in self-discovery and recovery from intergenerational trauma or other types of wounds, I hope that you feel encouraged to continue. In the words of the queen of Tejano music, Selena, "estoy muy excited" to share my story. This book is for brown women the rest of the world has tried—and failed—to conquer. It is for twenty- or thirty-year-old me, who wished I'd had a life madrina or comadre to share, learn, and grow with. A madrina or comadre is akin to a spiritual companion to a child or another woman. Madrina means godmother, and comadre literally means to co-mother. Becoming supportive of each other as chingonas is about the divine feminine power of mothering: a protective, nurturing, laboring, and caring relationship with one another. "The patriarchy pits us against one another in competition and feeds us the lie of scarcity," Karen González's podcast guest Jennifer Guerra Aldana reminds us. "What if we approached our comadrazgos fully supporting each other, knowing there's more than enough for all of us?"

We can all draw from each other's stories. Comunidad makes us stronger. This is what I hope this book offers you: a place among other chingonas en comunidad.

2

LA MUY MUY

Acknowledge the Soul Loss

Assuaging the psychic and emotional pain of subjects of trauma is an integral part of any decolonial project. . . . We are not split. We are infinitesimally interconnected with the whole of our environments, and therefore, must decolonize ourselves as we decolonize all parts of the cosmos.

—SARA A. RAMIREZ

"Tell me about a time you failed at something and how you handled it."

The interviewer's question hung in the air as I stared at the computer screen in front of me. Sitting on a high stool at a counter on the edge of the coffee shop, I paused to think. We were partway through the interview, and by now the sweat was collecting on my blouse's underarms. Underneath, I could feel my hot skin trapping moisture between my arms and the sides of my body. I removed my long cardigan sweater, wondering why I had even worn it. Moving my elbows away from the sides of my warm body and allowing my chest to expand wider and wider, I reminded myself: *Deep breath, Alma.* I fanned myself with my hands a few times. The coolness of the breath entering my lungs and the hot exhale dispersing into the humming fan above me brought immediate relief. The sweat drops on my forehead and lip became evident to me now that they sat on my much cooler skin. I ran my fingers across my face to collect the droplets as I stared at the screen in front of me.

From the corner of my eye, I could see someone else seeking privacy from the patio-style tables that lined the middle of the coffee shop. As the stranger climbed onto the high stool next to me to set up his computer on the bar desk facing the wall, I quickly glanced to acknowledge him. Then I pushed my headphones in as if to say, *This is a quiet space.* Seeing him and his fair skin manage to find not only this rincón in the hood of Boyle Heights but also the seat right next to me? Well, it felt just as jarring as the question.

Tell me about a time you failed at something and how you handled it: I knew the answer the interviewers wanted. Job interviewers want to know how we have overcome significant obstacles: what we did and what we learned from it. The mistake or failure is not so much the focus; it is always about how we handle it. What did you do to bounce back? How did you remedy the situation? What amazing qualities did you display in the face of defeat?

People, especially those in power, love hearing about those miracle moments—those times that someone had the foresight to act cool and collected while things were falling apart. They love stories of people who strategically turn the tide of history in their professional or personal life for the better. Give us a hero or a shero moment, a horrible experience transformed by ingenuity and grit.

Okay, I admit: the interviewer probably wasn't looking for that type of grandiose answer. At all. Still, I felt frustrated by the question and what it brought up in me. I knew they wanted at least a sweet story of overcoming obstacles and wrestling a failure into success.

But a nice little packaged story is not the kind of story I had for them then. It is not the story I have now. My story is a hard, chaotic, messy one. Perhaps yours is too. Chingonas have often endured much. Chingonas across time and space and cultures frequently have hard, chaotic stories. My story is messy in part because I had a lot to figure out on my own as a child, and I carried that trauma into adulthood.

But my story is uneven and not easily packaged also because to be a chingona is to be rebelde. Rebellious. When you are rebelde, you don't like rules. Rules sometimes seem unfair to you because at times they are actually unfair. But rules also seem unfair to you, the rebelde, because you are used to making your own.

I longed to tell the interviewers that their question—*tell me about a time you failed and how you handled it*—was loaded and simplistic. The truth was that I had such a story. But I knew that recounting it to them would leave me feeling raw and exposed. It would force me to continue the interview on the verge of tears and thus possibly forfeit the job altogether. Breaking down was not an option. The story I *could* have told them is a very personal one, filled with many long hours turned into days turned into years turned into decades. It is a long, messy story of challenging and sometimes ugly work on myself.

A time I failed and how I handled it? This job interview should have come with a trigger warning, I thought as I put my hair up in a top bun. I had worked so hard prior to that moment to feel more integrated and whole, and now it felt like I was being asked to split myself again. To give a packaged answer. To offer people in authority a carefully curated story neatly folded with a successful conclusion.

During what felt like about the same number of minutes it would take me to go from East Los Angeles to the west side of town, I carried on an internal conversation as I contemplated how to answer. I was trying to convince myself to make up an answer to the question. Give them what they wanted, hold back the rest. They don't want complete truth and vulnerability, I told myself; just give them the answer they're looking for. Just tell the story of a failure that had a happy ending, and then we could move on. I had those stories. But I was deep down a rabbit hole of questions about their question, and far into an inner dialogue about how upsetting it all was.

Here I was, with the interviewers waiting, and I knew I had to show up as my best "white professional self." Answering a question by asking another one did not seem quite right. What would they think about a candidate asking questions about the question? Yet I could not simply be silent either; I had to pull it together. It was rude not to respond.

So as the coffee bean grinder went off once again in the background and the smell of fresh-ground coffee filled the air, I came back from the spiraling scenarios and reminded myself, "This is it. *This* is the time to use small talk, to give a neatly folded, happy-ending answer." So I did.

THE MIND AND BODY SPLIT

I have disliked small talk for a long time. The world values shallow, quick responses that allow us to get on to the next item on our to-do list, and small talk skims the surface and ignores the wounds and joys and real things of life, in my not-so-humble opinion. So, earlier in my life I had resisted small talk, avoiding it when possible. In social situations, whenever I interrogated out loud the questions someone else asked rather than answering in pleasant and cooperative tones, I made others uncomfortable. So I learned to shut down that part of myself. I learned to leave that Alma behind—or at least keep her hidden.

But we cannot hide from ourselves. Sure, it was easier to question what people really meant or to problematize their words. But this only made me come across as la muy muy. It was my way of protecting myself from intimacy, from facing a deep psychic split. Somehow, I had learned to split my mind and body. I had worked hard to ignore the voice that was telling me there was something inherently wrong with me. To keep those thoughts at bay, I worked hard to prove them wrong. This also kept me from listening to my own body when I needed rest. The craziest thing is, others complimented me on my ability to keep going, to work so hard despite myself and be a type of superwoman. But I could no longer keep going with this mind-body split. Owning your inner chingona means acknowledging the psychic split so that you can begin to repair it and honor your body.

This is what this book is about: understanding the whole-body psychic-level healing that is needed. Many of us learned to hustle in order to survive, but finding mindbodyspirit healing requires acknowledging our frightened spirit: our chronic suffering from historical trauma. Some writers, including Elena Avila, author of *Woman Who Glows in the Dark*, have called this sense of fright "cultural susto," or "soul loss." They understand the historical and cultural roots of this split. They believe that our psychic split comes from intergenerational, systemic trauma: the results of colonization and the effects of the conquest of the Americas. And this is what I set out to understand through this book: not only how I came to this mindbodyspirit healing, but how I could come alongside others in this experience.

A night several years before the coffee shop job interview, I was interviewing for a different position: a professor position at a nearby university. The previous year, I had been an adjunct professor for the same university. I remember orientation day that year and how shitty I felt when I received a much thinner and less glossy orientation folder than the full-time faculty received. Soon it will be *me* holding that other folder, I promised myself—the one reserved for full-time professors.

The truth is, anger, competition, and discontent had fueled most of my drive and success up to this point in my life. From how I talked to myself to how I thought of others as simply getting in the way, competition and performance reigned. I prided myself in thinking I was accomplishing it all, alone. I was more able to keep it all together and under control than others around me—always ready for the next step. La muy muy. So full of myself. Convincing myself I was a big shot, that I was all that.

I had accepted the university's invitation to stay at a hotel near the university where I would be interviewing. Though it wasn't far from home and I debated the option, I opted for the peace and quiet of the hotel room and not being home with the kids to prepare myself for the next day. As I drew back the black-out curtains, the sheer overlay invited warmth into the otherwise bland and sterile khaki-hued room. I stood in front of the full-length mirror, examining my face and staring at my hands. This is what I often do during life's big moments. "I want to remember how I look, how old I am at this moment," I said to myself. It's a way of feeling more present with myself.

I had watched myself grow old in mirrors like this. I remembered watching mangoes ripen when I was a kid: slow, imperceptible, but somehow clear. The mangos we would pick at my abuelita's house in Mexico would ripen over days from a hard dark green to a soft yellow-orange to a fleshy red, until finally they would darken and bruise. I had watched myself grow older, but somehow I could no longer recognize myself. I felt an existential numbness while at the same time, my body continued on its slow journey to decomposition and decay of cells. The bacteria of continuous work eroded me.

The muffled sunset rays peeking through the sheer curtain landed gently on my face and arms. I stood motionless, feeling the warmth of it on my brown, always-more-wrinkly-than-before skin. For a second, I felt present. I remembered myself. I was inviting myself back.

But then, just as fast as a hummingbird disappears when you lay your eyes on it, that sense of wholeness was gone. Once again, I felt disconnected from myself. Numb. Split. Unsure of how to even listen to myself again.

I felt like the dismembered goddess of the moon, Coyolxauhqui. In Aztec mythology, when this goddess tried to kill her mother, her brother, Huitzilopochtli, the hummingbird god of war and the sun, got wildly infuriated. He decapitated Coyolxauhqui, throwing her head to the sky to become the moon and her body down a mountain, splitting her into many pieces. A large stone disk showing dismembered body parts commemorates Coyolxauhqui at the Templo Mayor's base in Tenochtitlan, Mexico.

In that moment at the hotel, standing before the mirror, I wasn't sure if I was Coyolxauhqui or Huitzilopochtli. I felt like both siblings: full of rage on the one hand, and broken on the other. I didn't recognize who I was, and I longed to put myself back together into a whole being.

It was one of many times I have felt split from my own body so tangibly. I felt dissociated, decapitated. It was like I was hovering above myself—a complete other entity judging my thoughts and my emotions rather than simply feeling or thinking them. It is very disorienting to feel split like this, to finally look around for an herida, a wound, you didn't know existed and that you cannot see. To all of a sudden not recognize yourself. To feel like an extra, rather than the protagonist, in your own story. The staleness of a dismembered entity. I had been a rebelde for so long—a rebel pretending nothing could hurt me. As a teenager I had taken this stance out of necessity for survival, but now that is all I knew how to be: a fighter, a loner, who only knew how to hustle and survive.

I had taken weeks to prepare and be ready for the interview the next day. Yet my body remained unconvinced and uncooperative in this new uncharted territory. "I don't belong here," I murmured, feeling like a foreigner in my own body. Maybe I *wasn't* prepared for this interview, I started to think. I wouldn't have minded being thrown off the sacred mountain about then. Being flung across the universe.

Perhaps I had not done all I could to take the edge off the nerves of that evening, I thought. So I went down the list of everything I'd done to relax for what felt like the millionth time, as if trying to convince myself again. I was starting to feel out of it. I had drunk a bit of wine—not too much that the sugar levels would keep me up, but enough to feel a bit buzzed and tired. I had listened quietly to meditative music, and I had taken deep, intentional breaths. I had even tried masturbating, which always seemed to work, though my mind was far too busy even to enjoy it or continue. Maybe I was just clueless, I thought. My mind was too far apart from my body.

I turned away from the mirror and rustled some papers out of my bag to look over before I went to bed. I reviewed the materials in an attempt to regain confidence in myself, to feel complete. I dropped the stark black-on-white text-filled pages on the nightstand. I knew what was on the pages. I groaned and then settled into bed, hoping that the weariness from the day would overtake me and that I would find rest.

Instead, however, I had a cold sweat all night long. My heart was pounding, and I could not stop going to the bathroom to relieve myself of what felt like all I had ever eaten and drunk my whole life. My stomach kept turning, and I could not fig- ure out why. All I knew was that I had felt this type of sleep- lessness before, in my mid- to late twenties. Back then I was used to running on four to six hours of sleep. It usually started as I settled in to bed, whether by myself or my latest fling. My mind was always racing, thinking of all the possible scenarios of what I needed to do the next day, week, or year. It usually started with remembering what I had not accomplished or not done "correctly" that day. It always ended with a deep sense of loss or grief. Regret mixed with loneliness. Meaninglessness.

Now here I was again, sleepless and mad at myself. Up to that point, I had believed that that interview was what I had worked for so hard for the last six years of my life: the rigors of graduate school classes, the hours of writing papers, the stress of studying for exams. "You did not go to a doctoral program to *not* be a professor," I told myself, lying in bed. "You are too old, and you've wasted too many years, to not at least try to do this full time." But I was so worked up that I was convinced I had already ruined it. "I *want* to be a professor," I told myself over and over again, mainly to convince myself.

In that way I spent hours trying to relax: tossing and turning, in a fight between my mind and body. I had worked so hard for many years, yet there was an emptiness I could not ignore. I felt a susto—a soul loss—within myself. My thoughts were finally loud enough for me to hear them, and I needed to listen to my spirit. Maybe it was the marginalization and oppression I had endured in graduate school that revived that psychic-level wound in my being—the cultural susto of my ancestors living within me. We needed protection. We needed to know it was safe and that we were going to be okay.

A part of me also knew what awaited me after the interview: more sleepless nights, a more brutal grind. Maybe I don't have it in me anymore, I heard myself think. Maybe I don't even want to be a professor. Necesito descansar.

For many years now, I had not thought at all about what I wanted. For many years, I had been scared to admit that I had no idea how I had gotten to where I was—or if I even wanted to be there.

WARNING SIGNS

Sometimes we convince ourselves that it is less painful to *not* acknowledge a problem than to face it head-on. We find it easy to pretend that if we work harder—even when we don't know what we are working toward or why—the pieces will put themselves together on their own. We think that we will finally accept ourselves when we accomplish that new thing, get that other job, or marry that person. Then, we think, we will have the life we want. Contentment is always at the next stage of life; it must be out there somewhere, we think, waiting to be found.

But it doesn't work that way, does it? Especially when there is great pain and trauma that we have not yet confronted, we will never find what we are looking for. And it definitely does not reside outside ourselves. Many of us can't even remember how long we have held onto these beliefs about identity and what life should look like. When did achieving academically and professionally become my whole identity? Or yours? When did we decide we would prove everyone wrong with our "success"? For how long have we neglected everything and everyone—including ourselves—to prove these points?

When our commitments to achievement and success are no longer serving us well, we have to be brave enough to face the invisible fracture. We must acknowledge the spiritual wound. We have to first heal the split by allowing a cicatriz—a scar—to form.

In the middle of the self-doubt and the dissociation between our minds and bodies, we often want so badly to make the act work. We want to ignore the fact that there is a problem, because it feels safer to do so. Owning your inner chingona means letting go of when and how this mindbodyspirit healing needs to take place. It means accepting the various parts of ourselves. When we are expected to be our best white professional selves, like La Malinche, the mother of mestizos, we must reclaim Malintzin. Malintzin: this was La Malinche's name before the conquest—before that young Nahua woman had to fully accommodate to colonial systems. Yes, we are La Malinche, the participant in systems of conquest and competition. But we are also Malintzin: the woman who is her own.

Finally, just as dawn broke, I admitted that I was nervous—but no longer about the interview itself. I was worried that I had just managed to sabotage myself by not getting any sleep. I wondered if, somehow, my body knew more than my mind did. Did I not want this job anymore, or had I believed it wasn't for me? Was I just nervous, or was I losing it? What was clear was that both my body and mind were now turning against me.

The small, faint, flickering streetlamps outside the window were now turned off, and the light from the sun turned the cloth blinds into a bright white canvas. I lay staring at the neutral-colored ceiling, finally feeling weariness overtake me. I began to entertain the idea of calling off the interview—just canceling, saying I couldn't go forward with it after all. But the part of me that couldn't let myself fail got up, showered, and put on her best professional clothes. Stiff and monochrome slacks to correct the way my hips naturally curve: check. A silky and smooth blouse that is neither too revealing nor cute: check. La Malinche was ready to go.

The other part of me fought back by putting on her big gold hoops, red lipstick, and thick, winged eyeliner.

The professional self packed the papers back into the bag.

The other self—the tough girl—folded up her sleeves to show the tattoos. That's right. This is all of me, she thought.

Was I the professional, monochromatic-slacks-wearing academic? Or the chola—the tough girl—whose first playground was a lush, tropical garden? I didn't know anymore. These contradictions had started to take over. I felt fake, not sure which part of me was more authentic than the other. I had no idea how to begin to understand, let alone reconcile all parts of myself. Like Malintzin, I felt fractured at my core.

Anger wouldn't let me quit—pase lo que pase. No matter what. Here comes the Saint of Split Identities. I didn't even know how to stop at this point in my life. You're not weak, I told myself. You just need to try harder. Even if you make an ass out of yourself, I thought, you are getting through this interview.

The professional me knew I would regret not having gone through the interview, and that settled it. The tattooed, red-lipsticked, big-hooped, and winged-eyelined other-me didn't even fight her back.

We don't always listen to our own warning signs—the subtle and not-so-subtle hints that something is not right. I was split in two by partaking in a system that meant to erase me. The psychic wound of white professionalism on my Latina subjectivity was deep, as I had started to see myself through the dualistic thinking of Western society. I was the non-white, poor female, never able to measure up to the white, rich, male standard. I had not yet acknowledged that wound. I knew I would crash at some point in the interview process. What I didn't realize was how soon into the day—nor how fast—it would happen.

The interview itself was a whole day's worth of meeting departmental staff, students, and faculty. I had to teach part of a mock class to students, deliver a talk to departmental staff, have a luncheon, and meet the departmental lead one-on-one. The mock lecture would have been easy if only my body had cooperated or if my mind hadn't been hijacked by susto. I don't fully remember all that happened. I do remember feeling like my brown, tattooed, red-lipsticked curvy body sharply contrasted with the uniform desks and chairs in the class. I remember wondering if I would get through this. (*You bet you will*, professional slacks and monochrome other-me said. *Failure is not an option.*)

I didn't understand what was wrong with me. My whole psyche was finally registering years of generational oppression and violence. Barely able to stay awake after a night of no sleep, and spiraling in and out of a state of panic, I could no longer sustain all my roles and identities. Mother, scholar, wife, researcher, sister, colleague, chola, activist, friend, daughter, spiritual person: could all those even coexist? There was something inherently wrong with me; my interviewers could certainly see right through me, I thought. I believed that they, too, would find out these irreconcilable parts of who I was.

When I think of the rest of that day, the memories come to me in flashes. After the presentation, we went off to lunch. By then I felt like a complete imposter: a fraud, so tiny and insecure. That good old friend and coping mechanism—anger—reared its head with a vengeance. During lunch, I sat across from people who I was convinced were nothing like me. *They* knew what they were talking about and what they were doing here, I thought, and that fact made me furious. I could feel myself starting to lose it, fast, and I needed to distract myself before I turned into the Aztec god of sun and war, Huitzilopochtli, myself.

Then it happened: one of the men interviewing me questioned my perspective. His question had to do with college access and the study of equity in the entry-to-college pipeline. My professional and academic life's work has been to promote college access for low-income people of color, as they are systematically underrepresented. I studied the barriers to equitable access for this population. "So what is your opinion about the future of higher education given the new technology-based economy?" he asked. "Will college degrees still be relevant?"

Looking back, I realize that this full-time professor wasn't actually disagreeing with me. Now I see that with that question he was throwing me an alley-oop. He probably wanted to help me. He was asking me to talk about a subject I was passionate about—college access—and on which I had opinions. He knew I cared about systemic change, and he was likely asking questions he thought would get me to talk, questions that would get me out of my head. But it was so hard for me to trust him—to trust anyone, including myself, at that point. I was accustomed to angrily fighting my way when I felt vulnerable. Are you kidding me? I thought. What kind of question is this? Out loud I gave a resolute answer. "Of course! Because certain students will still need degrees." No explanation, no elaboration. Inside, I was trying not to convince myself I deserved to be there. Silence filled the lunch table. I immediately realized how antagonistic my response sounded. La muy muy.

I had meant, of course, that no matter the structure of the economy, marginalized students would need avenues to power. As long as there is no systemic change to *who* holds power and the elitist paradigm that sets the agenda, those without power in our society have no other recourse than to abide by the rules of that system. I meant to point out that, while rich white kids with connections might not need college degrees anymore to get a good job, the rest of us still would. I meant to suggest how ironic it was that, just as people of color were gaining access to higher education and the professions that rely on it, the whole thing was perhaps becoming "irrelevant."

I didn't care anymore—or at least that is what I told myself so I wouldn't feel like a complete idiot. All the water I had been drinking to stay awake finally decided to avenge itself on my body, and I spent the rest of the lunch excusing myself to the restroom at least four different times. I never really recovered or rejoined the conversation.

I could not wait for lunch—and the entire day—to be over. By the time the day ended, with a final interview with the departmental lead, both the tattooed ex-chola and the monochromatic professional within me were done. Both La Malinche and Malintzin needed rest. I could not even get myself to answer the questions in the grand finale meeting.

Still, I had done it. I had kept my promise to get through the day even if I made an ass out of myself (and that I did). I had completed the interview. That day my mind and body fought so hard I would never again be able to ignore it, the deep spiritual wound of susto. I had crossed a new threshold into utter numbness. It would get worse—much worse—before I could regain a sense of confianza in myself again.

SOUL WORK

What do you do when you are not spiritually or emotionally prepared for any next step in your life? What happens when you neglect your needs for so long that you have no inroads on how to find them? Who do you become when you trade your sense of self for white professionalism or academic success—and how do you coexist with the person you've become due to those decisions? What happens when years of an overwhelmingly busy life turn into numbness and then, sometimes, into hatred and shame for who you have become?

That evening when I arrived home, my husband dragged me and the kids out to celebrate. He was sure I'd get the position. I knew he was proud of me, and I watched my then two-year-old and twelve-year-old smile proudly too, as if this stage meant Mommy was done working so hard. My husband and I sat on benches, having greasy burgers and beer, and our girls ran around on artificial turf in front of us, their hearts full and pure. Their joy felt just as cold to me as the steel walls of the pop-up hipster kitchens surrounding us in the outdoor food court. I felt like a stranger watching a family celebrate. I could not wait to go home from what felt like a pretend celebration and rest.

As I walked through the doorway of our home, brown wicker baskets, my red couch, and a dimly lit, dark-wood-paneled living room wall warmly welcomed me back home. The worn sheets on my bed wrapped my body in a familiar embrace. I had had too much greasy food and beer and heard a ringing in my ear. I touched the right side of my face, my cheek tingling, feeling like thick wax.

As my body began to relax, my mind was still active and conscious, fighting sleep. I felt my spirit depart from my body: susto. It stood hovering over my body, watching me sleep. Terrified, I tried to get up, to wake myself up multiple times. My mind was still panicking. I knew I was asleep and was aware that I couldn't get up, yet a separate part of me was trying to come alive. It had no time to pretend everything was okay.

I didn't know it then, as that diagnosis would come much later, but this experience, known as sleep paralysis, is common in those with complex posttraumatic stress disorder. I still didn't know how the fight between the many parts of me would impact my whole being, how I would still need years of work to reclaim my mindbodyspirit health. That night, the soul work that I needed still lay ahead of me. I had ignored some serious signs and had lost sight of what life was about, what the struggle was for, and it would take years to recover that vision.

Sometimes we have been at odds with our bodies and minds for so long that we can't even remember the last time we felt peace and completeness. Though I finally fell asleep that night, my mind, body, and spirit had kept score of all I had put them through over the years. I had to find out who I really was and to be whole again. It was time to heal the wound.

LEAVING BEHIND LA MUY MUY

For years I was bitter about that "failed" interview—and no, I didn't get the job. Yet now all I think about is what a gift that day was because it forced me to acknowledge the wound I had been carrying for far too long. On that day my body and mind decided to fight back: to reclaim wholeness and authenticity, my chingonaness. To find a different type of coraje: the nerve to fight fears.

I did, however, get the job that I interviewed for at the coffee shop several years later. I sometimes still wonder, though, if it's because I gave them what they wanted to hear: the neat and tidy version of the previous job interview story.

I wanted to make up a story so badly when that interviewer said, "Tell me about a time you failed at something and how you handled it." But how do you feign failure? And why make up something when your whole body intimately remembers the real thing: a sleepless night, a disastrous interview, a split and wounded part of oneself that refuses to be ignored?

So I ended up telling that interviewer the partial truth, the polished story, in measured tones. I described the time I interviewed for a professor position and how "despite not getting the job, I didn't let that stop me from recreating my career trajectory." It sounded so ludicrous. *When did I start talking like this?* I asked myself as soon as I said it. *Where I come from, you don't just say things like that.* But I heard myself continue: "I went back to my community work roots instead, working directly with low-income, college-aspiring youth of color, and I loved doing that. And I get to leverage my role there and side hustles to find a way to still teach and lead future leaders."

It hurt even to hear myself say this aloud, but of course it's what they wanted to hear. The victor's story. *Some* truth, *some* vulnerability. Never mind that it was the most watered-down version of the most challenging moment that turned the tide of my professional and personal history.

Maybe it was the hot green tea I chose to order instead of the much more caffeinated iced drink I needed, or perhaps it was the hot, dry Los Angeles summer day that made my face hot all over again. I placed my hand on my face, my index finger right below my nose, pretending I was still in deep thought, though I mainly wanted to wipe the sweat off my upper lip again. My body was remembering the split.

So, I got that job. And like I said, my shero story was partially true. The absolute truth was much more gut-wrenching and a painful catalyst that would take me many years to accept.

We fight so hard sometimes to admit the obvious. We have difficulty surrendering ourselves to what the spirit has to show us, what ancestral wisdom through our own bodies is telling us. How do we reconcile all our identities? How do we heal the split—the spiritual wound we do not want to see?

To own our inner chingona, we need to leave la muy muy behind. We need to acknowledge the many wounds of our past and our present. We must choose to be brave not by becoming numb but by accepting what the wound is here to teach us. We need to forgive what La Malinche had to do for survival and hustle, and we need to tell Malintzin that she is safe, protected, and loved.

3

NEW LANDS, NEW HOODS

Go Back Where Memories Lead

The stories we tell about our lives shape what we're able to imagine, and what we can imagine determines what we can do. My job is to change the stories we tell and help us imagine a world where greed has no power, the earth is cherished and all people get to live safe and satisfying lives. Because once we truly imagine it, the pull to create it becomes irresistible.

—AURORA LEVINS MORALES

From the time my mother started working when she was a teenager, survival was all she knew. As a young woman in Acapulco, Mexico, she had first worked in a panadería, making pan dulce. I wonder sometimes what it would have been like to smell the fluffy sweet cinnamon dough on her, how long it lingered on her young brown skin.

I wonder, too, how survival smelled for her when she left Mexico in the 1980s to start a new life in a country to the north. I imagine her new life in the United States as full of hope, adventure, and love. Still, being pregnant for the first time in a foreign country and far away from her family must have brought up so much fear for her. Everything familiar was now gone: her body, her country, her life.

Then, when my mother married my father and got pregnant with me in that new country, I wonder what survival looked like. She gave birth to my sister three years later and was soon pregnant with my brother. I wonder how she worked through her pregnancies and postpartum experiences on her own. Like so many migrant women who move to a new place, she persevered, for years, despite an inhospitable political and social climate. Immigrant women hang onto the edges of the economy, surviving in jobs and situations that many people would find untenable. These women are chingonas in their own right: sacrificing and persevering in the midst of extreme challenges and outright xenophobia.

After her marriage ended, my mother had to go back to work to provide for us, and it was simply impossible to do so while caring for three young children. Survival meant finding a way to earn money as a single parent. Like many women who return to work to provide for their families, she dropped us off with our grandparents while she went back to work.

Except work was in another country.

And it would take her years to pick us back up.

THE NEED TO REMEMBER

Sometimes we are eager and ready to step into our chingona journey. At other times, challenges and circumstances force us into it. For me, it took a sense of dismemberment of my body and mind, a schism in my being, to prompt me to embark on a journey to claim my inner chingona. It took years of waking up from vivid, disturbing dreams—dreams full of feelings so strong they would hijack my brain and bring back painful memories—to realize that memory is a crucial dimension of the chingona journey. Memory holds the power to slowly build up fear within us. Memories that remain unhealed can make us give up hope for the world and the people in it.

At times we can't even recall memories or bring them to the surface—our waking minds simply find them too painful. Instead, we feel the pain through our bodies and imaginations: body aches, tense breaths, and vivid dreams. We may try to avoid anything that would remind us of the pain and suffering of our childhoods, especially thinking and talking about it. These memories can bring up so much misery that our brains actively work to erase them.

Over time, I've learned to manage all these memories better. Owning your inner chingona means confronting painful memories and being brave enough to ask yourself hard questions. What did this suffering come to teach me? How has all this pain helped shape the person I am today?

These are new lands for many of us. I like to think of this place of remembering as a new hood I'm living in, a place of soul care. A place of growth my ancestors worked so hard for me to have. Memories give me access to a still place within me, where I can fully embody my emotions and surrender to myself. Going to where our memories lead helps us surrender and accept all the experiences, feelings, thoughts, and dreams we've had. In my case, that has meant trusting, holding, and being present with the little girl in me who was abandoned. Learning to hold her and love her.

Owning our inner chingona requires noticing deep spiritual wounds from our childhoods. Moving through the pain and darkness in our lives can refuel us to have more capacity for faith and joy. Before we can heal, we need to remember.

PALMA SOLA

When I was four years old, my mother left me and my sister in the care of my grandparents in Palma Sola, Acapulco, Mexico, so that she could return north to work. My mother wasn't sure how to leave behind her kids, especially me, since at age four, I was old enough to understand that she was leaving. So after we arrived at my abuelita's house in Palma Sola, she made up a story that she thought would make it easier for me—and perhaps her—to say goodbye. She was going to go down to the store to get me a paleta, she told me, and she would be back soon.

Later that day I must have found it strange that she still had not returned with my popsicle. I must have been confused and scared, wondering if she would ever return. When my grandmother finally told me that evening that my mother had left to go back to the United States, she wasn't sentimental about it; it was just a matter-of-fact bit of information, offered on a need-to-know basis. It wasn't until my eyes welled up that my abuelita's own eyes filled with tears. It must have been hard for my abuelita to see her daughter leave this way, without her children, headed back to a new land.

To be honest, I'm not sure which loss I felt more keenly at that point—a paleta or my mother. Most likely it was both. I was in shock. When my mother first left, I certainly didn't understand what her absence would mean. But eventually I must have gathered that it would be a while before she returned, since many of my cousins were also living there with my grandparents. My tias, their mothers, were also working in the States. So this wasn't my grandmother's first rodeo. She had taken care of plenty of children, including eight of her own and now many of her grandchildren, both Mexican- and US-born.

Having plenty of playmates reassured me for a while. My cousins and I were all still so full of hope, wonder, and imagination. While we sensed our mothers' absences, the concept of time and hurt had not yet fully entered our consciousness.

During my mother's absence, which would stretch four years, I spent my days running around barefoot on a lush garden surrounded by fresh almond fruit, grosella berries, and lime and mango trees. I sat for hours watching particles of rain dance in the sun's rays that shone through our barred glassless windows. I remember the vivid fuchsia bugambilia that adorned our neighbor's fence. Sometimes, if it rained hard enough, tiny frogs, still with tail fins, would appear on the unpaved floor inside the house. If I stood still enough on the muddy pebbles and small rocks, the frogs would begin to climb between my toes and onto my ankles and legs. I loved watching their bright green bodies try to climb up, and then slowly slide down, my sunlit brown skin. I loved holding them in my hands and collecting them in jars. Then I'd watch them as they'd climb out over the rim, ever so slowly.

My cousins' preferred activity was climbing onto the flat concrete roof of our grandparents' house. This allowed them to stand next to the mango tree to pluck the fruit. Then they'd eat those freshly picked, unripe green mangoes with sal de grano, a thick, coarse sea salt, and salsa búfalo, a hot sauce that bit the tongue. I wasn't supposed to climb up the stairs onto the roof, and frankly, neither were my cousins. But as we grew older, my grandmother was often too busy bottle-feeding my siblings, and my grandfather and uncle were either too distracted or still at work. So my cousins and I would secretly climb up the forbidden stairs to the roof. We loved dangling our feet off the concrete rooftop, eating green mangoes with salted hot sauce to our hearts' content.

In Mexico, when school was in session, I would walk with my best friend up and down lush green hills to get to our elementary school. At the back of the school there was a beautiful ravine, and palm trees enclosed the playground. My friend and I would walk home together in the afternoon, the ocean's coastline coming into focus as we hiked the hill back home.

EMBODIED FAITH

Despite the company of my cousins and my friends and the natural beauty of our surroundings, my heart longed for my mother. I ached for her presence whenever I wasn't busy, and as I grew older, I grew more aware of her absence. Each time she called or sent gifts was a reminder of her absence. Usually, when the Tres Reyes Magos were set to arrive with gifts during holidays, I asked to have a "real" family. This tradition—of being bestowed with gifts that supposedly came from the wise men and that recognized the birth of Jesus—made Christmas feel extra special. But my prayer remained unanswered.

My first encounter with the divine was through my abuelita's shrine for the Virgen de Guadalupe, the mother of God, which was displayed right in the middle of our long rectangular common living space. She faithfully tended to that shrine, bringing freshly picked chamomile, cempasuchitl, and lilies and keeping the candles lit. I watched her in front of her shrine multiple times a day as she whispered and made the sign of the cross, pointing her fingers across her own body before sealing it with a kiss. Her spiritual disciplines were embodied ones, as regular and faithful as the rain during sunny days in Acapulco.

Maybe my grandmother found comfort in the mother of God because she could relate to her agony. Imagine carrying love and hope so close to you, literally in your body. Imagine, then, surrendering your child and having faith that it's what you must do to continue having that same love and faith.

That's what my grandmother and the Virgencita taught me: to let go, to surrender love and hope and joy, and to believe that giving up these things is the very way to experience them. I don't know what my grandmother meditated on as she diligently tended to that shrine, but I think it had to do with memory and surrender and love.

The Christmas holiday always marked another year my mother had been gone. But each year I was also reminded of the Virgin Mary, and her strength brought me comfort. To this day I find strength and comfort in the faith that Mary, my abuelita, and my mother had. I embrace the impossible idea that even as we surrender our hope and love—and even our children—to the world, we are still able to practice joy.

The Virgin Mary in my abuelita's shrine, with her beautiful dark brown hair and eyebrows highlighting the depth of her brown eyes, reminded me of my mother. Sometimes during those years I imagined what it would be like to be as extraordinary as Jesus. I imagined my mother looking over me like the Virgencita looked over the infant Christ, with tenderness and fear and hope.

MOTHER WOUNDS

My mother came back to Mexico to get me when I was almost eight years old. When I went back to the United States with her, without my siblings, we lived in South Central Los Angeles, where Martin Luther King and Jefferson Boulevard meet. That is where my mother and I first lived together again. We slept in a bed set up in the living room of a one-bedroom apartment that my uncle and aunt rented.

I wish I could say that her physical absence during those four years was the hardest challenge our relationship would have to overcome. But it wasn't. I don't know when, but at some point in her life, my mother disconnected from her own ability to fully live life undistracted and in wonder. She had given up hope and love for so long that I don't think she knew how to reclaim it. It's all she could do to let go of the pain, to just survive.

How was she to survive in this new land? I imagine she decided that disconnection from the pain was the only route to survival. Except once we disconnect from the pain, we also disconnect from the joy around us. It's as if my mother had lost faith, her strength. As I acclimated to my new life in the States, after having been so far from her for half my life, I wanted to know if my mother still loved me even after all that time apart. I wanted to ask her questions all the time about her life, her work, what she had done during the years we were apart, her love for me. But my questions brought so much agony in her that she would fall silent, sometimes for days. So I stopped asking.

Now, looking back, I wish my mother would have fought through the tears to allow herself to come out the other end filled with a wider capacity to hold pain while also holding love and hope. I can imagine this potential only because I too had to learn to do this. Before I was ready to face the pain of memory, though, I spent years working to cut off emotionally, to ignore and forget the four-year-old me that was left behind.

On the outside, I was living the quintessential Mexican American life. Or so I thought. Not the overly proud, multigenerational Chicana, low-rider car-riding, Tex-Mex food-eating kind of life you see on TV. But the daughter of immigrants, with only Spanish syndicated television and radio playing in the background, getting money wired *from* America before coming *to* America— that kind of life. Many of my peers understood this life.

That year, I was in second grade. Before I was even into the school year a few months, there had already been a couple of drive-by shootings in homes right next to the elementary school I attended. Each time a shooting happened, we had to duck down or lie down on the playground blacktop. Each time, my clothes would get ruined with soot and dirt.

Frankly, while living in Mexico, I had expected more from the land in el Norte. When I was young, I imagined the place where my mother lived, where I would be reunited with her again, as a place of safety. But now in the States, I frequently felt afraid and alone as I walked the harsh streets of South Central LA.

I don't remember speaking very often that year. I did not speak the language of my new peers and teachers. Though some of them spoke Spanish, I was the new, different kid. Only a few months into living in this strange new land, I had my first fistfight. A boy had just beaten me at tetherball. I managed to kick him in his balls for being the first person to beat me at this game. It was not him winning that made me upset— although that stung. It was him laughing and pointing at me while speaking words I did not understand. So I kicked him, and he returned the favor and kicked me right back between my legs. It hurt—but I wasn't teased again that year in either Spanish or English.

I do remember doing a lot of staring that year. I had no idea what the adults or kids around me were saying, and I felt left behind in a completely new way. I watched their mouths carefully and conjectured as to what they could have been saying. At times, I found myself reminiscing about my old, lush playground in Palma Sola, about my big family and close friends there. Sometimes I wished I could climb up a techo and find myself again in the coastline, palm trees, and colors of my previous home.

During that first year in the States, I also received lots of tests at school that required me to get pulled out of class often. They must have found an adult who spoke Spanish to administer the tests. I still don't know exactly what those tests were screening for, although I imagine they were psychological assessments of some kind. Those tests recently came up in a conversation with my husband, when I asked him if he had ever been screened at school. I asked whether the adults had ever shown him images that looked like comic strips of different people, all in black and white, and asked him about the little people and how he thought they were feeling. That's what happened to me, I told him, remembering the loneliness of those little cartoon characters and the forlorn feeling I got when I looked at them. "I think they were all sad," I said.

My husband cocked his head and widened his eyes, waiting for me to get it. Slowly it dawned on me. I realized *they* were not sad; *I* must have been the sad one. And I remembered thinking every picture the adults showed me seemed to be of people finding out bad news. Some of those people in the pictures even made me teary. I remember black inkblots on sheets of paper, and adults asking what they made me think of. And then they showed me a watch—and let me tell you, that one *really* made me cry.

Sitting there as a kid in an empty classroom in South Central, with adults trying to help me, I thought about the passage of time. I thought about how long it had been since I had left my home—or what I knew of home up until that point in my life. Everything familiar was gone: running barefoot on unpaved streets; the lime, almendra, and mango trees that greeted me each morning; waking up to the comforting warmth of humid, hot weather with a cool ocean breeze; the sound of my abuelita's broom methodically sweeping away the old day to greet the new.

I missed everything: the neighbors' roosters crowing right as morning broke and the colorful birds that seemed to chirp back at them. The boulders I loved to climb right outside my front door. It seemed I had traded all that for a dirty, violent, concrete playground with metal poles. Everything familiar was now gone.

LIFE IN LOS ÁNGELES

We moved to Boyle Heights the next year. Although this city in East Los Angeles was where I had been born, it was just as unfamiliar to me at that time as South Central had been. That year, I picked up some English and new ways of making friends. Each morning before walking to school, I stopped at the nearby Tianguis supermarket on the corner of Sixth and Soto Streets to steal candies for me and my new friends. I learned that if I paid for one or two candies, no one seemed to realize I was taking more in my backpack.

Back when I was living in Mexico, my grandparents had converted the front room of our house to a tiendita, where we sold all kinds of snacks, candies, and drinks. I would regularly earn the right to claim a candy or two for helping out around the little store. But I would also secretly always take one or two more than was intended. Taking more than what I paid for from stores did not seem like a big deal to me. No one ever seemed to notice, not my grandparents then or other store-owners now.

My newfound friends in the States were shocked at how generous I was, but my new teacher wasn't too excited about our increasing energy levels in the classroom. Ms. Quirarte, a slender and well-traveled older Filipina woman, was the first person to ever tell me I was smart. She was also onto how I was procuring so much candy for my classmates. Surprised I had not yet been caught stealing, she knew I had been doing it to elicit the friendship of my peers. So rather than shame me, she pulled me aside one day and told me that if I directed my mind and efforts toward something other than shoplifting, I, too, could one day travel to as many places as she boasted of.

Thinking back, I wonder if she saw how unattainable and far-fetched her life sounded to me. Maybe she knew how stubborn and determined I was when I set out to do something, and that I simply needed a vision of a life beyond what I knew. Either way, that year I grew closer to Ms. Quirarte, my first true friend in the States. She challenged me to see myself through her eyes and to focus in school. I wanted nothing more than to make her proud. For the first time since arriving in this new land, I felt the warmth and comfort of someone welcoming and reassuring me. She gave me hope that I would find rest here.

The next year came with even more changes. My mother told me my sister was on her way back from Mexico. Seeing my sister after two years without her in my life felt a lot like seeing a close friend after years of losing touch. I immediately embraced her when she arrived, and she felt like a complete stranger in my arms, much like my mother had felt to me just two years earlier. I felt so distant from her.

My sister's arrival also meant we had to move again. All three of us were sharing a room in a two-bedroom apartment in Boyle Heights. We lived with an aunt and uncle, a different pair who had just had their first child. This was the year we moved to Huntington Park—otherwise referred to by my siblings and I as we got older as "*Ranch*-ington Park" because of the high population of Mexican immigrants who lived there, especially in the 1990s. Huntington Park is a lot more diverse and includes many Centroamericanos as well as other mainly working-class populations. In some ways it didn't feel much different than Mexico to me because everyone spoke Spanish and all the signs around the city were in Spanish. It was still hard for me to see what was so magical about this country, though.

Having my sister with us comforted me. Everything happened fast, but I had started to get used to the constant changes. All of us—my mother, sister, aunt, uncle, and primo—moved to a large two-bedroom house before the start of the next school year. When we moved to Huntington Park, my sister attended the local elementary school, but due to overenrollment in my grade, I was bused to a different school. After spending years in different countries, we were separated again. I felt this separation was unfair, but that was a feeling I was starting to accept.

Over the span of the next ten years, my family would move four different times. Each time, our moves were within a mile radius, from the corner of State Street and Florence Avenue and Gage and Salt Lake Avenue. We started and ended on Hood Street. Yes, Hood Street, as if it wasn't enough that we clearly lived in the hood, we also managed to live on a street named Hood. This made for lots of great jokes—most of the time ones we came up with ourselves.

After a couple of years of living in Huntington Park, my mother was doing well enough financially to afford to rent her own place. We would finally have our own home. Although an older cousin moved in with us to help with bills, everything seemed to be falling into place. There were serious talks about my brother joining us soon too.

My mother had been dating, and soon she got remarried. I finally had a reunited family, a new sense of home in this new country. My brother joined us about the same time that my mother remarried. So before I got the chance to get to know either my stepfather or my brother, whom I hadn't seen for five years, we were suddenly a whole unit, a newly formed family.

"No seas un espejo, solo el reflejo de con quién andas" was one of the very first lessons my stepfather taught me: Don't be a mirror, a mere reflection of those around you. When I first heard those words, I wasn't sure what they meant. That year I had joined a gang and those words rang like a warning, a threat. Maybe he had figured out my new allegiance. He had stopped letting me use the phone at night. "Whatever!" I'd say, pretending his rules didn't hurt or affect me and trying to convince myself that I didn't care. I wondered whether he knew those evening phone calls were when we made plans to skip school.

My stepfather's other favorite saying during my teenage years was "Dime con quién andas y te diré quien eres"—essentially: we are a reflection of the company we keep. I mean, what *is* a gang but a group of kids trying to find acceptance by looking and acting the same? The whole goal as cholas is to look alike, blend in, find belonging. To be a mirror to each other. Like me, my new friends had found a new family to be a part of. Maybe they, too, were disillusioned with their families. Maybe my stepfather was so angry because I was finding acceptance and connection outside of our newly formed family.

The further I pushed away my stepfather and others and began to do things my own way, the more they wanted to make me follow their rules. Yet as much as I tried to define myself against my stepfather, I am also a lot like him. I, too, want to convince others to see things my way. I hate being told what to do, but I have to constantly remind myself to not tell *others* what to do.

I understand my stepfather better now. Sometimes I think about his inability to lead from his own brokenness. How he tried to demean and yell me out of my stubbornness rather than telling me about his own pain. I wonder why he was so angry and what he was so scared of. The anger and fear he held onto kept us in bondage for years. We replayed the abuse he himself had endured as a child. My stepfather was still a scared, confused, and unloved little boy. Yet he was also now a parent. After I grew up and these years in the hood were past, I would have to fight hard, emotionally and spiritually, to reclaim myself. I would have to learn to reparent myself, reassure myself that the painful journey would be worth it.

As chingonas, we often have different work to do than our parents. I don't blame my mother for what she did in those years—all the choices she had to make, the people she had to rely on, the ways she had to cross into different lands and relocate again and again. Like Malintzin, the Nahua woman who is the mother of mestizos, my mother made the compromises necessary for us survive. Her life's work was simply a different one than mine. She toiled physically, traveling across borders and taking us to new lands. My labor has been different. Yet I, too, have toiled to take myself and my own children into new spiritual and emotional lands.

Vivid and often upsetting dreams have been given to me throughout my life. I frequently dream of bodies of water, troubled and vast. One night when I was in my late thirties, a dream surfaced for me the abandonment, distrust, and anger I felt at that time of life. The dream also spoke the promise of joy and hope. Through this dream, I began to understand the wound that has remained with me since childhood, and to remember how that wound first came to be. It helped me remember how I lost the sense of hope, awe, and wonder I once held.

A DREAM

In the dream, I am with my mother and stepfather and sister and brother, standing on volcanic rock at the edge of a black sea. Murky, tar-like fluid is dropping off at the edge and into the water. I watch as both my mother and sister dive into the black water and swim toward an island in the distance, covered in a colorful abundance of mangoes, cocos, and plantains. My mother makes it onto the island. Although she struggles to get across the water, she is immediately out of sight once she reaches the shore of the island. When and how my sister gets across is less clear, though I know I don't need to worry about her. She will be okay.

I am longing to be on the other side of the black sea, with the women of my family who have already reached the island. With that all-seeing, ever-present consciousness of a dream, I can see the island in great detail. I notice glistening red, gold, and translucent jeweled rocks sprouting up from the lush green garden floor far off on the island. Multifaceted crystals of all sizes sprout up from the soil. Overhead, a dark green canopy of tree branches and leaves shields the warm soil. On that island there is calm and shade and perfect warm weather.

The tropical island stands directly to the north, and it looks inviting. It will offer relief from the dark, cold, and unpredictable place where my stepfather and brother and I still stand. Its presence enhances the uncertainty I feel. It's an unattainable paradise, and I feel fear when I realize how far away it is.

My stepfather and I are both scared, frozen in place, surrounded by darkness. We are arguing. I sense that our turn to swim across the black sea is coming soon. We both know this, but we are also frightened to swim. So we focus on my brother, who is entering the water. He seems to struggle as he swims away, and the more I doubt my own abilities and fear the journey, the more he struggles with his strokes. We are connected, and my fear is keeping him from reaching the island.

In that dreamscape, my stepdad and I are also as if one entity. I can sometimes see him, and other times I *am* him. In one moment I am cheering on my brother as he swims, and then suddenly I am shaming him to get across. "What is wrong with you? You don't know what you are doing! You will never get across that way," the stepfather-me entity declares.

Now my dream consciousness shifts once again, and my brother and I begin to become one. He—or we—are almost there, to the island on the other side of the black sea. As he swims, I simultaneously feel the joy of almost reaching the other side of the water with him and the horror that he may not make it— that he might surrender to the water and give into the darkness surrounding him. My brother begins to lose strength and hope and starts to think he won't make it. No one seems to notice his struggle to get to the other side.

But I can, as he and I are one now. We have joined consciousness, and we sense a flat rock lying just inches underneath the surface of the water. But no matter how much we try, we can't reach it with our feet. Back-on-the-rock me tries to will the sludgy waters to drain so that we can see what is underneath. It seems that beneath the sea is something bigger—a structure that is supporting us all. A foundation beneath all the fear and striving. If we can just trust that, we will be secure and safely held, we will have reached it: the beauty and protection of the island.

My brother is so close to the island now. He is covered in black tar and moving slowly but steadily. As I watch, I long for him to experience getting there, to a better tomorrow. I long for him to reach a place of safety, to set his feet on the teal-green garden that will offer him comfort and rest. But we cannot trust the process or the destination. As soon as we are confident we will make it to the island oasis, we fear the darkness of the water and the movement toward something unknown.

WAKING UP TO THE DEEP PSYCHIC WOUND

As I woke from my dream, my arm lay on top of the sheet and comforter, exposed and cold in the middle of the bed. In the moments right before I awoke, I had the sensation that the events were speeding up. I'm not sure whether I snapped awake because my consciousness sped up the dream to see it through to the end, or whether the intense feelings of anger, distrust, and abandonment had awakened me. I woke up with a familiar feeling, a coldness: the feeling that no one understood or cared about what had happened to me or us. The familiar feeling in my dream carried over to my waking state.

I lay there in bed, recalling when my mother left me in Acapulco after my biological father had left her. A deep sense of abandonment filled me even now, as a grown woman lying awake in the darkness. It was part of the spiritual wound I had carried for so long.

Groggy, I tried to understand what the volcanic rock on which I perched symbolized. Was it keeping me safe or simply holding me back? Why was I so angry at my stepdad and at myself? And why did I need to keep protecting my brother and looking out for my sister? I lay there, analyzing the very familiar feelings from my dream, wishing I knew how the dream would have ended if I hadn't woken up. Would my stepfather and I make it past the darkness and onto the tropical island? Would my brother? And why did no one else but me notice or care to help my brother? Did my brother represent me?

How small his body, I thought; my brother must have been eight or nine years old in the dream. Though my own age in the dream wasn't clear, I would have been twelve or thirteen at that time. Those are about the ages we were when we reunited, after years of growing up separately. When he arrived in the States, it felt more like the first time we met.

As I lay there analyzing, I realized that in real life, as in my dream, each family member came separately to the north. When I was young and living in South Central Los Angeles, I was sure that *someday* I would start to understand just how special this place was. Maybe once the rest of my family—my sister and brother—were brought back from Mexico, I would feel that sense of completeness. The promise of a better tomorrow, arrival to the beautiful island oasis in my dream, felt ever closer. Except my newly formed family didn't turn out to be the magical place I had been longing for.

It had been a long time since I had seen my brother and stepfather in the same space, I realized, as I thought of the dream I had just had. The last time my whole family was in the same place at the same time had been almost a decade ago, probably

at a christening or some other major family event. Thankfully
we've come a long way since the time of my dream, meeting
up and celebrating more milestones together. But back then,
when I had this dream, we were in the middle of many years
of separation between the men in my family, and my sleeping
mind was trying to make sense of it all. From the time my
mother took me to stay with my grandparents in Mexico, to
the time she brought me back to the United States, to the time
my sister and then my brother arrived, to the time she married my stepfather: through it all I imagined what a reunion
would look like. I thought this reunion would offer protection
and security. Instead, I ended up feeling misunderstood and
disconnected from all of them as we struggled to survive in
LA in the 1990s, some of the hardest years for immigrants in
California.

Fear and stubbornness kept my stepfather and I arguing on
that black rock in my dream, I realized. We directed our
anger at each other instead of seeing what we were losing. We
couldn't handle the shock of it all: the shock of this cold, violent, new land, this new hood. My own familiar world was
gone: the mango trees, the frogs, the rocks, the ravine, the roof,
the jungle, and La Virgencita. Perhaps my stepfather's known
world was gone too. Stuck, he was standing at the edge of that
black rock in my dream with me—also scared, confused, and

unloved. Stuck re-creating a familiar type of parenthood and childhood.

What we both wanted was to feel that warmth again, the comfort of the home our childhood minds created despite the pain we also experienced. Yet we were unable to reach a place of rest and comfort with each other. A safe and loving home. We longed to be a part of something beautiful together, but we were stranded.

By the time I had this dream, I had already given up on this new land, on the idea of ever having the type of family that would offer me love and joy. I knew there was no magical place, for like my stepfather, I, too, had lost faith. There was so much fear, pain, and anger those years. My disillusionment and deep sorrow—upon realizing that the magical new country or the kind new stepfather or the happy reunited family would never exist—were murky, tar-like, and always threatened to overwhelm me. To swim toward the love and joy of a nurturing home, an island of belonging with others—I could try, but who is to say I would make it?

So there I lay, trying to make sense of the dream. I replayed it over and over, hoping that something in the dream—or in my past—would change. Except it never did. I was in that liminal state between sleep and wakefulness, my heart racing, when suddenly, warmth radiated onto my arm, a reminder of the present. My husband's touch finally brought me back to the present moment, to the bedroom where we lay. I took a deep breath, and another and another. You cannot change what has already happened, I told myself. You can only remember it and accept it.

It is true that as chingonas, we must always practice faith in a new day. Yes, we must make our way toward a vision of a better future. But owning our inner chingona also requires noticing deep spiritual wounds from our childhoods. Before we can heal, we also need to remember.

In my dream, as in my life, my mother never really looks back. Her destination is survival. How distant I feel from her as I watch her emerge from the dark sea. In the dream she struggles, at first, to plant both her feet onto the lush soil of the island. But once she has made it onto that magical oasis, she shakes the oily black fluid off her body. She stands up and straightens her back. Then she disappears into the canopy of trees.

4

THE "MOST MISERABLE CITY"

Insist on Telling Your Own Story

There's really no such thing as the "voiceless."
There are only the deliberately silenced, or the
preferably unheard.

—ARUNDHATI ROY

According to a recent news article, I grew up in one of the "most miserable cities" in the United States. The city in which I spent all my teen years—Huntington Park—is actually ranked top in the state of California and tenth in the nation.

I was nine years old when we first arrived in the southeastern part of Los Angeles, where Huntington Park is located, and I wouldn't leave this side of town again until I moved to the west side of the city, at the age of nineteen, for college. I don't remember feeling ashamed of living here until that move. But once I moved out, my goal quickly became to leave the hood behind and never return.

And while I hadn't exactly felt shame about living in Huntington Park, I admit that there were times during my youth when it felt like I was indeed growing up in the worst place ever. When I first read the article about the most miserable cities in the United States, I was relieved to find out Huntington Park wasn't ranked at the very top. In fact, for many years, my ability to afford living in places *not* like the one in which I had grown up felt like true success. If I could live anywhere else but a neighborhood high on some business magazine's "miserable city" index—well, I felt like I had made it.

Yet the greater the distance I had from the hood in which I'd grown up, the greater my appreciation grew: for what that place had afforded me and for who I had become while I lived there. Not only did the neighborhoods of my childhood and youth make it possible for my family to survive financially, they enabled our physical survival. We needed an affordable place, and one that insulated us from more dangerous neighborhoods. In the 1990s, it was not easy for brown kids like us to avoid gang life. In Los Angeles during that era, living to the age of thirty made you a veteran—an OG. The life expectancy for a brown kid was not very long.

I now have a strong sense of pride that I once lived in Huntington Park. Though I never returned, I am grateful for Huntington Park, the place I referred to as home for a long time. Owning your inner chingona means not only accepting where you come from but learning to actually love it. No matter how challenging or "miserable" others consider them to be, the places that shaped us make us who we are today. Part of my chingona journey has meant learning the sociocultural history of my home. It's easier to love where you are from when you learn the truth about it and its complicated "misery."

In fact, the beautiful thing about reclaiming your own origin story is that you learn the root causes of not only your sufrimiento but of your resilience, and you learn that others are not as different from you as you once thought. You begin to see the ways you are connected to other people living in places that powerful people consider "miserable."

A COMPLICATED MISERY

In the 1990s when we lived in Huntington Park, I watched as it turned into "Little Mexico," a cultural enclave. Previously, at another point in its history, Huntington Park had been a suburban hub for a strictly white community. From its inception in the 1900s, Huntington Park had an ideal location in the "Gateway Cities" district, between Orange County and downtown Los Angeles, which made it a convenient locale for white commuters to live in. Lured in part by an elaborate trolley system (before the government's divestment from public transportation), residents had flocked there for years to work in the manufacturing industry.

Like many places in the United States, the city was redlined in the 1950s—that is, financial and other services to Black and brown communities were systematically denied in such a way as to increase residential segregation. Banks wouldn't loan to buyers in these neighborhoods, deeming Black and brown communities too "high risk." This primarily anti-Black racist practice was meant to separate the surrounding Black communities of Watts and South LA and to provide work predominantly to white folks in the cities of Vernon and Commerce, where many production factories still stand to this day. After the outsourcing of industrial production, which started in the 1970s, Huntington Park experienced many economic downturns. By the mid-1990s, a combination of these factors led to almost complete white flight. Given their ultimate inability to keep Black and brown kids away from Huntington Park schools, white families fled the city.

But white flight is not the only reason there was almost complete demographic turnover in the enclave. In the mid-1960s the Fair Housing Act allowed some Black and brown people to buy and rent property more freely instead of being limited to certain pockets of the city by the Federal Housing Administration's racist redlining practices. When various neighborhood populations were shifting and whites fled, the prices of houses were then too high for most Black and brown populations surrounding Huntington Park. During this time, the city of Watts, down the street from Huntington Park, saw the biggest uprising of the time, rooted in a clash in housing demand and supply, high unemployment rates, and racist policies. What are sometimes called the Watts "riots" took place in August 1965, as the desperation and frustration reached a fever pitch. All this contributed to the "misery" index of Huntington Park over time, I'm sure.

As white working- and middle-class folks were leaving the area, upwardly mobile and multifamily Latine households like mine were moving in from East Los Angeles, from Mexico, and from Central American countries. When we first moved to Huntington Park, my neighbor Steve would be one of the last white kids to live on my block. I was bused to an elementary school in Watts; there, too, my best friend, Shannon, would be one of the last white kids in my school. It was 1992, I was in fourth grade, and we were less than five miles from the epicenter of the biggest racial rebellion LA had ever seen: the uprisings in the aftermath of the Rodney King verdict. The verdict, in which white police officers were acquitted of using excessive force on an unarmed Black man that had been clearly caught on camera, was the catalyst for the LA uprisings. Both Steve and Shannon moved shortly after the verdict.

When a magazine creates a "miserable city" index, none of the causes of its misery are included—only the symptoms. Median household income, percentage of residents living in poverty, population change, and percentage of persons without health insurance—these are some of the data points the article uses for its so-called misery index. But what about the actions of mortgage companies and law enforcement and local government? Who will hold them accountable? Where's the index that assesses their culpability?

Owning our inner chingona means learning to imagine a world where we don't blame victims—one where we instead hold leaders accountable for the law and policies and practices that have caused so much harm. Growing up in a working-class community like Huntington Park—being poor, having limited access to healthcare services, and needing to move multiple times—was difficult. But it was home. My inner chingona will not let others distill my experience down to a single harrowing word. In that sense, I want to be an unruly woman: one who will not let a number on an index of misery define my home.

Miserable? No. I'd say complicated. The most complicated city in California.

LEARNING TO BE A REBELDE

When I first arrived in Huntington Park in the early 1990s, I lived smack-dab in the middle of Mexican Mafia–controlled territory. Florencia Trece was the main gang in the part of Huntington Park to which we had moved. Since I was bused to an elementary school that went to the sixth grade near Watts, I was surrounded by Crips and Blood gangs, which were reserved for African Americans. In that way, I avoided prime recruitment time for Florencia Trece. This was not the case for many of my Latine peers who were hit up in late elementary and early junior high years to join the local gangs. At the time I wasn't aware of street politics in this way; I was just learning to fight for my survival. I was also starting to embrace being a rebelde.

I thought it silly that rival Latino gangs were fighting with one another and that Black and brown people were too. Especially after seeing the treatment of Black and Latine protestors after the Rodney King trial verdict, I thought it strange that Black and brown youth couldn't find a way to unite our interests. Deep down in our bones, I think, we knew we had more in common, even if we hadn't learned it yet.

In the middle of my survival behaviors, I had a hunger for life and knowledge. Upon my arrival to this new school, I clung onto a white girl, Shannon. We were such an unlikely pair, but her extroverted and protective demeanor made sense alongside my distrust of people and tendency to retreat into silence. Once her family moved away and she was gone, I started noticing boys for the first time. Not knowing what to do with the attraction and feelings I felt, I often lashed out at unsuspecting crushes or rivals. Being 140 pounds and five feet, two inches by the time fourth grade rolled around made me a perfect rebelde-in-training, and people's responses to my body only fueled my resistance to established norms and standards. My body itself was a transgression against those standards. Once, while standing in line to go back to class after recess, a boy made fun of my fully developed body. I slapped him several times. Afterward, a classmate stood up to me. She would have hit me right back if I had done that to her, she said. As she walked back to her place in line, I heard her whisper to someone that I was a bitch.

I actually liked that girl's response. It was a language I understood. She and I were both trying to make sense of an order we had nothing to do with creating. We didn't know any other way to live except to rebel against whoever was in charge and had set the rules. Standing up for yourself was a way to do that. You had to take charge, and you had to "not take shit from anyone" (whatever that means). I don't think I fully even understood these concepts, but they were already a part of who I was.

By the time I was eleven years old, I had already made vows to not trust others and not let others hurt me. "Hurt or get hurt" seemed to be the only rule governing the streets between Watts and Huntington Park, and I had decided I would not be hurt. It was just a matter of time before others tried to hurt me, I figured, so I did everything I could to protect myself— even if it meant hurting others first and going against those in authority.

Part of learning to love where and what we come from means becoming aware of the pacts we made with ourselves when we were growing up. When we are young, we often make promises to ourselves—who we'll be, what we won't do—as a way to survive our environments. That was the case for me. What promises did we tell ourselves very early on in life, and how do we bring complexity to those promises? Yes, my pact with myself is what got me through at the time, but does it serve me still?

Not surprisingly, the classmate who stood up to me that day would soon become my friend. It was smart to become allies with other rebeldes. We felt stronger together, unstoppable.

Girl politics in the hood are complicated and often played out in small slights and subtle offenses. But little can stop you from owning your inner chingona like focusing on trifling things. Finding other rebeldes was very much a part of my journey.

Through my new friend, word got out about who I had a crush on. To be honest, I didn't mind. I responded to the news that she'd told others about my crush not in a "How dare you tell my business!" way but with "Whew, I'm glad I didn't have to do that—thanks, girl!" I liked the safety of distance from others when these types of feelings were involved. This didn't stop other girls who also had a crush on the same boy from confronting me, though. Apparently my first crush was highly coveted.

Many of us were trying to create our own type of order: to feel safe, protected, and loved. The attempt to survive can take away these things so early in the lives of some kids. Needless to say, I got into some fistfights that year, sometimes with African American girls at my school who were being recruited to rival gangs of Florencia Trece, the gang that ran the neighborhood I was bused from. Thankfully we still didn't know what all that meant. The fights weren't fair, because I was always so much bigger and stronger than the girls I fought.

But I didn't care. I couldn't care. I had already made a pact to hurt or be hurt. I had so much unexpressed anger and rage built up from years feeling misunderstood and learning how to survive.

WHAT DOES TOUGH MEAN?

My mother's side of the family—my five tias and their families—lived spread out across South and Southeast Los Angeles. Somehow my cousins and I all narrowly escaped extreme gang involvement, which was a bit of a miracle in the 1990s for Mexican youth in this part of LA.

We all had the makings of future cholos and cholas: Chicano and Chicana youth who become absorbed by gangs. Our parents were living in poverty and had to work long hours, which left many of us unattended after school. There was hatred and rejection of our changing communities, which showed up in cross-cultural conflict between Black and Latine populations. There were constant sexual transgressions and physical violence in our families and groups of friends. Alcohol and drug use prevailed among our parents, though it was never openly admitted. Rather, it was understood as a way to relax with one another at the latest weekend "pari." Those gatherings were time to unwind after a week of brutal, laborious work.

Those get-togethers were how we found out what was going on in each of our families. Through the highly elaborate and secretive chisme train—gossip passed mainly in hushed, hurried conversations between my tias—we found out information: so-and-so's dad had raped them, so-and-so's tia had bruises, and so-and-so's cousins were found doing drugs. These were different from your typical family chismes; we had beyond-telenovela-level chisme. The stories passed around were sad but, unfortunately, less and less shocking over time.

As much as these stories normalized violence and substance abuse for me, even then I hated how transactional it all seemed. Why was this information all so secretive? And why were the women in my family so ready to tolerate abuse? Why were they not dreaming of change or a different way to live? Why was it hard for them to be tough? To resist power and find their own sense of safety? Over time I learned to hate what I saw in the women of my family. I disliked what I could only understand then as weakness. It was hard to tolerate or understand their choices to stay in toxic and abusive relationships. If any of them were truly tough, I reasoned, they would get out of their situations altogether. Some of them did, but some stayed. The ones who stayed made me angry. I wondered when they, too, would get angry enough to demand something different of themselves and others.

Back then, I didn't know much about intergenerational trauma. I didn't realize how hard-fought their current level of freedom was. To simply be surviving in a country that denied and exploited their existence as immigrant women? That took a measure of toughness I couldn't yet see. I couldn't see how brave they had been to have left the only country they knew, some of them as teenagers, or how much they were figuring out on their own, as path pavers and resilient warriors.

Back then, all I could aim for was a refusal to become another chisme tale in my family. I would never allow them to have anything to say about *me*, I thought. Yet even as I thought this, I, too, was becoming hardened. I was becoming unable to accept and love myself enough to be vulnerable.

WHO TELLS THE STORY

In 1992, after the LA uprisings, I first truly understood the importance of who gets to tell the story and that storytelling is not neutral. The story changes depending on who is telling it. And who gets to tell the story has a lot to do with power and with our imagined realities of each other.

A story can be used to otherize or bring us closer to each other. In her now-famous TED Talk, novelist Chimamanda Ngozi Adichie warns of the danger of "the single story." Our stories need texture and an acknowledgment of complexity about ourselves and each other. Owning your inner chingona is about reclaiming your roots by telling your own story. We will only be free when, as Aurora Levins Morales writes, we are "able to insist on our own stories about who we are."

My tias frequently talked about the interracial conflict in our neighborhoods. So-and-so got dragged by "un negro" when she wouldn't give up her purse; so-and-so shouldn't go to that Black neighborhood; so-and-so lives near "morenos." It was clear, in their minds, that I should steer clear of Black people. But this would prove hard for me. Avoiding Black people was not possible, as I was bused to Watts, a historically Black neighborhood, for school. So at school, my African American teachers and peers were all I knew, while at home my tias and Spanish news stations were all saying that Black people are "dangerous" and that, to stay safe, we must avoid them.

This isn't something I am proud to say about my family, but it's true. And the dissonance I saw—between the lives of Black people I knew and the stories my family and the media told about them—was the beginning of an awakening and paradigm shift for me. I couldn't help but see the parallels between my Black friends' families and my own. And what did my family's anti-Black racism mean about us? My family, like many Latine households, struggled with colorism, and we were complicit with Indigenous and Black erasure within our communities. The ideal standard was measured by our proximity to whiteness. Whether we were considered beautiful had a lot to do with our facial features and hair texture and how much *less* Indigenous or Black we looked than other cousins, families, or communities. Despite growing up near the Costa Chica de Guerrero, a part of Mexico with one of the highest Black populations, and having Indigenous and Afrodescendiente roots, my family lived with this racial tension.

The stories my family chose to believe and retell were those of the little privilege they had garnered by distancing themselves from their Blackness and Indigeneity. I get it. Aligning ourselves with Spanish stories and reminding ourselves of our proximity to European ideals seemed a more tolerable and less painful narrative than seeing our connections with Black and Indigenous relatives. Still, it separated us from those with whom we had so much in common.

Meanwhile, I was learning how to question the "single story." All three years I was bused to Watts, I was taught by African American women. My teachers clearly loved what they did. They always noticed when I was too hungry or tired to perform at the level they expected. They took care of our basic needs as students, offering us snacks when it was clear we hadn't had breakfast. They made sure we were ready to learn their stories.

Before college, very few teachers of mine gave assignments that elicited my opinion or understanding or nurtured critical thinking. Usually education, in my schools, meant rote memorization and regurgitation of white history. But two of my teachers in Watts, Ms. White and Ms. Hawkins, demanded that I show up with my own voice. They asked us to read various newspapers and interpret *how* the story of the LA uprisings—what a lot of folks still call the "riots"—were covered, not just *what* was covered. In one article, the violent looting and rioting that occurred were positioned as instigated by Black people. Another article told the deeper hurt and source of the anger—a justice system that could acquit four white officers who had savagely beat a Black motorist almost to death. I learned to ask *why* questions about stories. Why is this story being told this way? Is imagining this reality something I am being convinced of or invited into?

There is so much power given to who tells the story. Through this assignment, I learned that storytelling is not neutral, and I also understood it so personally because I lived it. You lash out at others and you hurt others because they hurt you. When they have hurt you for so long, it penetrates to the core of who you are and how you define yourself. Or you hurt them before they hurt you, because it's going to happen—they are going to hurt you eventually. This is what I believed. This is the story I told myself. This is not what my teachers wanted me to learn, of course, but it was what I already knew. What they wanted me to see was that the uprisings were more than what some media sources made them out to be. Black folks had their own families, maybe even with similar issues as mine. They were full humans, not just angry and violent ones. Through their teaching, I began to imagine that I, too, could learn to tell myself a different story about others.

Ms. Hawkins and Ms. White both showed up for me those years in a way I didn't know I needed. They took care of me and nurtured my intellectual needs—and they did it in a way that was loving and affirming but also direct and unapologetic. They didn't agree with some of my choices outside the classroom, but they also didn't victimize me. They made me rise to the academic challenges they set for me despite the more readily available trajectory into chola life. They were mentors as I learned the real history and root issues in my community. They helped me understand that sometimes the effect and the cause—the symptom and the source—were more interrelated than the fairy tales on TV made it seem.

Through these teachers, I learned that owning our inner chingona requires interrogating the stories we hear. It means diving deeper than what we are told by one source.

CHOLA SPIRIT

By the time I transitioned to my local middle school in Huntington Park, La Eme—which controlled most Latino gangs in this and other parts of LA—had laid some ground rules to limit cross-Latino gang conflict. Seeing how much African American gangs were financially benefiting from crack money, the Mexican Mafia set up a system to tax drug dealers through local gangs under their purview. Taxes in the street economy extended to other street vendors, miqueros, and even churches in exchange for protection. It was not uncommon for youth to get taxed for the new shoes or tech gear they had. Fights between Latino gangs became rare, but they still happened. Growing up in this environment meant I had to either take my chances without protection or join a local gang and survive.

Mexican American gangs have roots in racial stereotyping and discrimination—they are themselves a survival strategy. Finding a subculture or alternative culture to belong to when you are not welcomed into the mainstream culture is about survival. When communities are systematically denied work and home-buying opportunities, they create a street economy. Not being accepted for how you dress and act further alienates and fuels the fire of rebeldía and resistance. It is no wonder that by the 1990s in Huntington Park, I had a number of gangs to choose from when I wanted protection and to learn to survive.

Being friends with gang members made you "affiliated." Of course, I didn't fully understand this back then, but I did want protection, and hanging around cholas, the girls who belonged to gangs, seemed like a good option. One day the girls decided to "jump" me and make it official. This was my very short-lived stint as a chola.

When the head of our set saw my grades, she mocked me for being a nerd. I told her that my stepfather would kill me if I came home with bad grades. Her response shot a pang of guilt right to my gut. "Wait. Your father *cares* what grades you have?" she asked. I had assumed all parents cared about grades—or maybe if not about grades, in particular, surely about who we were becoming and what choices we were making. Of course my stepfather cared! He constantly reminded me of the privilege I had of getting an education—one, I was quick to remind him (mostly in my own thoughts), I didn't ask for. He had started working as a young boy in Mexico and had to drop out of school to help make ends meet at home. He had loved school and regretted not being able to continue. He made it his personal mission to see me and my siblings go further in school than he had.

I wondered what her parents were like and realized in that moment that I barely knew her. She seemed confident, and she was bold enough to be a gang leader. I had assumed she had entered that life willingly or with purpose, but now I wasn't too sure. Many kids are born to gang life due to generational involvement. She must have been equally confused by my life. She couldn't understand how someone's parents would want them to get good grades and aspire to a different life and legacy than their own. "If I had those grades, I wouldn't be in a gang," she said.

Her reasoning made sense, but all I felt at the moment was rejection. Even the cholas didn't want me. After a few more months, she let me walk out of the gang. There would be no "jump out" rites, no savage passage to earn my freedom.

But before I was allowed to walk out, I had a significant experience that resulted from being in a gang. I sometimes wonder whether that incident actually saved my life. It all started when my chola friends and I had broken into the teachers' lounge at school. We spray-painted graffiti over the walls. I had been dubbed "La Happy" when I joined the set because of the closed-mouth, barely visible half-smile I showed when I was indeed happy. My nickname was sarcastic—an attempt to make me actually smile and laugh by pointing out how much I sucked at looking "happy." I owned it, though. It really resonated, both the barely-there smile I carried for years and the humor about it. At that time, I liked my name so much I decided to tag it all over the teachers' lounge. So while some of my newfound friends in the gang wrote their names as inconspicuously as possible, I used a black spray can and wrote "La Happy" across a wall.

Believe it or not, that choice—spraying "La Happy" on the wall—likely saved my life. The middle school teachers and other school administrators were so mad about the vandalism in the lounge—especially about this *happy* one who had declared herself so boldly in black paint—that they brought in the Los Angeles Police Department's community resources division and started pulling known gang members out of class. They'd scare them straight by threatening them with jail time or other dire consequences until someone told them who "La Happy" was. They were narrowing down their search toward me, and I was so scared of getting found out.

By the time they got to me, they were ready. The police officers told me I had been ratted out by someone who was there with me that day in the lounge. I felt betrayed. Both the police officers and my school counselor, Ms. Barns, knew I had just joined the gang recently. They also knew I was likely informed of the upcoming rumble with a rival gang.

When they threatened to call my parents unless I gave them more information about the planned fight, I dared them to. I knew there would be no parent answering on the other end;

my parents were at work and wouldn't be home to answer that call during school hours. This was well before cell phones were readily available, and I had purposely omitted any work numbers from school forms.

On my way home that day, our set leader showed me a pile of guns stashed in a car trunk for the upcoming rumble. There were guns of different types and sizes spread out before us, and I was scared. I was so scared, and while I usually didn't admit my feelings to myself during those years, I knew I was scared even at that time.

Looking at that stash of guns, I felt like I was already looking at my life in past tense. There is no going back once you use a gun on someone, and I couldn't even imagine doing so. I know now that I wasn't the only one scared. We were thirteen- and fourteen-year-old children. Back then we didn't even have first-person shooter videogames to help us practice or during which to feign bravado. All of us, especially the younger recruits, were definitely in over our heads.

The next day I spent all day in the school's main office with the school counselor, Ms. Barns. I realize now that Ms. Barns kept me in her office so that I would not be at the rumble that was happening. Ms. Barns asked me a lot of questions that day. Was I made for this life? Could I really live a life of fighting? It all seemed like too much, and for what purpose? What would I really gain from it all? It's not like I'd never received those questions before from adults in my life who were concerned about me. The difference was that Ms. Barns waited for me to answer. She wanted an actual response. She wanted to understand me and my reasoning, and she wasn't just asking these questions rhetorically.

There was something genuine about Ms. Barns's queries. Maybe she was aware of the pain and hurt of kids who were playing with guns. She was a Black woman, and maybe she reminded me of my caring elementary school teachers. Or maybe it was just the words she spoke to me that day that made me reconsider my silence and refusal to cooperate. Whatever it was, her eyes let me know she could see past my hard exterior, meant to protect myself and hide how scared and lost I truly felt. I saw how much she still believed there was something else in me. Somehow she wasn't callused and hardened by seeing yet another aspiring cholo or chola in her office. She believed there was more to me. More to all of us.

Ms. Barns and I spent a few days together because I refused to keep the chisme train going. I wasn't going to tell on the others in the gang even if I had been (presumably) betrayed by them. And *she* wasn't going to let me go until I gave her real answers or at least until I had really thought deeply about what I was doing. She made me journal when I couldn't or wouldn't talk to her. She also looked at my school files and told me I had been designated as gifted in the third grade.

After a few days in her office, I was allowed to resume classes. I didn't suffer any other consequences. I was warned though, that the next time the school would press charges. We were all closely monitored during school, especially during breaks, to ensure we weren't hanging out with each other and conspiring.

Being in a gang had given me a sense of safety that I had not yet felt in my life. It had allowed me to start exploring who I was, why I was. I felt seen. When I was no longer in the gang, I felt a bit lost in the unbelonging my new freedom brought.

I now understand what a huge moment that was in my own development as a chingona, as someone who is learning to love her own story and reclaim her roots. Sometimes I wonder: What would have happened if I hadn't joined the gang? What would my life have become if I had not let out years of anger, rage, distrust, and loneliness on the walls of the teachers' lounge? Or if Ms. Barns had not kept watch over me during that rumble? What might have happened if I had pointed a gun on someone? Would I have fired?

Even though I was no longer in the gang, I still kept the chola spirit. I still try to. To me, keeping the chola spirit means lifting up others, like the leader of my set did when she believed in my future possibilities. It means fighting my way to finding my inner chingona. Keeping the chola spirit is also about finding your own way in a world that disenfranchises you and denies your very existence. It's about staying unruly, in all the best ways. It's about survival, yes. But it's also about *survivance*, which Gerald Vizenor, writer and enrolled member of the Minnesota Chippewa tribe, says is "an active resistance and repudiation of dominance." Survivance is survival with a chola spirit.

The following year, Ms. Barns died. Her life had meant a lot to gangsters, nerds, and gangster-nerds like me. She had played a pivotal role in helping me learn to love my story. I didn't know what to do with the pain of her death, so I wrote. I wrote about her, and then I surprised myself by reading what I wrote out loud to others. I auditioned to be the eighth-grade commencement speaker, and had I been awarded the role, I would have talked about what Ms. Barns did for me. I lost by half a point against the valedictorian. But the role of Ms. Barns in our lives continued to resonate within many of us for years after we left middle school. Though I never got to thank her personally, just auditioning to be the commencement speaker felt cathartic. It was my way of grieving, and I found belonging in that shared misery with others as we mourned Ms. Barns's death together.

Reclaiming our roots is about loving what made us the chingonas we are today—the trajectory to defining our lives for ourselves. Chingonas can learn to love their story when those around them love them for who they are. We can learn to question the way others tell our stories when it does not sit well with our lived experiences or the history we know to be true. Owning our inner chingona means accepting the complicated histories of our lives, families, and communities. Our stories are filled with lucha and survivance. This means that while pain is a part of our stories, it does not define who we are. Chingonas are coconspirators against the "single story" of history. We learn to dig deeper and expect more. Stories can help us grow stronger and remind each other of our complexity, and they have the power to pull us together.

5

LIVING IN NEPANTLA

Become a Cultural Coyote

If the fundamental outcome of colonized identity is self-hatred, then the [one] who can achieve self-love is closer to her liberation.

—TERESA CORDOVA

Eventually we must awaken to the ways that we ourselves are complicit in a colonial mindset. We need to reckon with the ways that colonialism has infiltrated the core of our beings, with how we have allowed ourselves to devalue our histories and see ourselves as inferior, less than, or inadequate. It can be difficult to admit how deeply colonialism has seeped into our own consciousness. What norms and expectations of a colonial mindset have we taken for granted without even knowing it? How have we linked our worth to the view others hold of us? Why do we feel like imposters? Why do we struggle to know contentment with ourselves? What conveyor belt of colonial thoughts and attitudes are you on, and where does it lead?

Because here's the truth: there is a *reason* many of us feel incompetent, "fake," or less-than, despite all our hard work and accomplishments. The belief that our worth is inherently linked to our accomplishments, or that we don't really belong in leadership positions, or that if people knew who we *really* are, they wouldn't listen to us after all: these beliefs don't just appear out of thin air. They have a source. It's been called imposter syndrome or imposterism and imposter phenomenon. For chingonas, this feeling of intense inadequacy is the result of a matrix of power, of systems that deem us to be unworthy no matter our competence, success, hard work, or leadership.

The deep source of imposter phenomenon for chingonas is the legacy of colonialism. The tension or sense of unease chingonas sometimes feel are part and parcel of colonialism. "Confronted with the colonial order, the colonized subject is in a permanent state of tension," writes Frantz Fanon, a French West Indian psychiatrist and philosopher. "The muscles of the colonized are always tensed." Our ancestors, whether they were colonizers or the colonized or both, lived in systems of violence, oppression, and dominance, and they left behind for us the inferiority and superiority complexes of our communal history.

Imposter phenomenon affects some of us more than others. Perhaps your parents or guardians lived in a colonized mindset, always trying to be something they were not or prove their worthiness. Or perhaps you were born into a situation where elders and caretakers had already awakened to the fact that this way of thinking was holding them back from being their true selves.

Even those of us who have awakened to colonizer influences on our imaginations sometimes revert to harmful ways of thinking about ourselves. This happens whenever we return to a sense that we're imposters—that we really don't belong in new spaces or positions of authority and power. When we do that, we allow ourselves to be complicit with colonialism. To accept the status quo.

But we are the generation of change agents. Chingonas are unruly women who break those cycles of thinking and being, moving beyond the fray and chaos left behind in our minds from violent pasts. A chingona journey entails understanding our complicity with systems that harm us and understanding all the ways we have done violence to ourselves by denying parts of ourselves and trying to fit a mold.

Thankfully, there is another legacy that our ancestors left behind for us. It's a legacy of survival, courage, and hope. A legacy of living in in-between spaces and of healing with and through our communities. It's a legacy of border-crossing—of becoming cultural coyotes, people who ferry others across difficult terrain and toward liberation. We, too, can lead in such a way that carries other people with us. This requires embracing all of our own histories and awakening to contentment with ourselves.

We have the potential to define our own legacy. Owning your inner chingona means becoming a new kind of leader, one who exercises leadership in inclusive ways that do not reenact violence and abuse. Chingonas do not bow to power or abuse it, but subvert it. Rather than accepting circumstances as defeat, chingonas see the limited options we are given—and then see beyond them.

CONVEYOR BELTS

In middle school, after I got dumped by the chola squad and after Ms. Barns died, I had an increasingly hard time feeling rooted or confident. Who was I, and where was I headed? Finding my own way as a young adult meant lots of conscious and unconscious decisions. It meant seeing two options for my life and being satisfied with neither one.

Through school and on my journey from adolescence toward adulthood, I was becoming familiar with the conveyor belt of the American dream, the myth of meritocracy, colorblindness, and "equal" opportunity. I was learning the story we are all fed through our schools' overt and hidden curricula: that whiteness rules the world and has done so for millennia, that we who are not white can achieve this power and status only insofar as we work hard, forget our pasts, and prioritize appropriately. This is the path toward the status quo—the conveyor belt toward true success. For me, academic achievement was a way out of what I thought was a predestined chola life, one that I had come to fear.

But I was always uneasy about what this conveyor belt asked of me: to let go of not only my family, history, and culture but also myself. I longed for a path that would allow me to become truer to myself. I could be focused in school and work toward academic success and become a perfect Mexican American daughter—but then, I thought, I'd have to give up my chola spirit: the fight within me to question and revolt against systems of oppression that upheld white supremacy, colonialism, and patriarchal systems.

The other conveyor belt to which I had access would mean following in the footsteps of my chola friends. I longed for their confidence, their self-assurance. They were the first leaders I admired. They were not leaders because others deemed them so; they were leaders despite what others thought of them. I admired that. My months as a chola had taught me the value of digging deeper and thinking more critically, which started my trajectory into finding my rootedness. The cholas were not just cholas; we were also smart. We were not just settling; we were also leading. The leader of my set helped me believe I could do more. She became my first mentor, seeing past my current circumstances and experiences and pointing me toward a different path. She was a change agent. Rather than being told what to do and how to dress by adults and authorities, we created spaces of resistance: to have our own style, defy unfair rules, and lead in our own way. Whether misguided or not, we were making moves toward our own liberation from controlling and repressive systems. We were walking toward new and unknown lands and identities.

Yet this conveyor belt that cholas had access to likely meant getting boo'd up, getting pregnant early, dropping out of school but also having lots of fun in the process. This path meant moving toward settling, which was something I couldn't understand. That is what was hardest for me to accept: the settled feeling. It would require me to stop and just be: accept my past, my current reality, and the unknown to where I was headed. The cholas around me seemed content with their choices, but I didn't believe that they were. How could they be? *I* wasn't. I was scared.

So as I considered which route to reject—the American dream or the chola reality—I had a lonely feeling, a sense of in-betweenness. To accept one of these paths meant I needed to reject the other. I could not be a nerd and a chola, right? There was no nerd-chola conveyor belt as far as I could tell—no predesignated "smart chola" path. What would that even look like? I could either be smart *or* a chola.

Having watched the conveyor belts for a while, I began to wonder: Why did the cholas drop out? Why did the nerds accept what was taught in school? *Could* I be smart and a chola at the same time? As I watched, I began to notice others who also didn't fit into any of the predesignated conveyor belts of life. The class clowns, for example: they were often the smartest ones in class, upstaging the teacher with their quippy responses. I was often compared to the class clowns. Humor was a way I, too, coped with how dismal my life chances seemed at that time. Teachers sometimes accused us of "not trying hard enough." But I disagree. We *were* trying hard: to test the limits of the status quo. Being funny or performing or trying to make others laugh—these were ways to escape the sadness, the brokenness we felt at the thought of having to choose either path but not both or neither.

The class clown, the chola-nerd: we wanted more than either of the conveyor belts offered us. We wanted to live in our complexities, or to at least not feel broken in a system not meant for us. We wanted to keep moving so we could find our thing.

For most of high school and college, I kept myself busy on the "American dream" conveyor belt of earning achievement to cash in for self-worth. We live in a world where grind culture makes us believe overworking is not only justifiable but honorable. Saying no to some things so we can say yes to others is not valued. We don't give ourselves time to pause and reflect. In college I mastered my self-imposed "work hard, play hard" calling. I didn't know how to be content with who I was and what I had already accomplished; my mind was constantly working up another goal to achieve. I was out of balance and unrooted. Recently I was looking back at all the awards and accolades I received in school, all that I worked for and had accomplished in my academic and professional career. Some of them didn't even make sense. I once received awards for completely conflicting goals: one for working closely in the community in which I grew up, the other for preparation to become a national leader, which would leave me with little interaction within my own community.

While I was still on the path to success, I met others like me, other chingonas who scoffed at conveyor belts while remaining unaware that they, too, were very much on one. We had so much to prove to ourselves as we traveled along on the status-quo belt—and we were really good at all that was required of us. Trying to prove we were worthy, we were defying rest and peace in our fight to belong.

I now know that this was all internalized colonialism. After people have been colonized, they don't suddenly shake off the colonial mentality when they become independent. After all, the systems that colonization created are still present; we can change legacies of the past only when we admit they are still here. While I don't like to admit how long I unconsciously accepted the terms of colonialism in those years—how much I felt I had to prove my worth to the system that oppressed me—accepting that time is an integral part of owning my story. Reflecting on that time in my life offers me the opportunity for self-compassion, to love myself all over again and to empathize with others on their own journeys to self-acceptance.

Slowly, over time, I was recognizing myself as a chola-turned-scholar, but I still didn't know what that might mean. It was not until I discovered a group of powerful chingonas who had reclaimed the term *chola* that it dawned on me that I could be both.

"You can't spell *scholar* without *chola*": that was the catchphrase popularized by a group of young high school girls enrolled in an ethnic studies course at East Los Angeles College, my alma mater. While the phrase has its origins among program members at the College of Education at the University of Nevada, Las Vegas, those high schoolers and many Latinas within other academic communities find it to be a source of pride. So many of us know the ways that the word *chola* has been used to denigrate working-class, Indigenous, or mixed-heritage Latina women. *Chola* has become a derogatory term, as have *cha-chas*, *chongas*, and *paisas*. Realizing that the word *chola* was literally embedded in the term *scholar* was so freeing. Looking back, I see now that reclaiming *chola* was such a chingona move: to reclaim an identity that has been used against us. I know now that this chola spirit I thought I had to give up—the energy of defying systems that harm people, rejecting the status quo—could actually stay alive within me. In fact, this very identity was encased within my new identity as a sCHOLAr.

As a young adult, I didn't realize that this sense of in-betweenness—of not fitting on one specific conveyor belt—is what leaders often feel: that there is no predesignated path for them, no conveyor belt wide enough to hold all of who they are and what they want the world to be. These leaders often have to create new paths, new tracks, toward new destinations. I didn't know it then, but I was learning to live in the in-betweenness that many often find themselves in, especially those of us who are the first in our families and communities to find a different path and open that path for others.

BOTTLE IT, SELL IT, AND GET RICH

When I was in tenth grade, a school counselor asked me how I had gone from failing most of my ninth-grade classes to receiving straight As in advanced and honors courses the next year. While I didn't have an answer for her then, I know the answer now, and it's one that might surprise you if you value academic achievement: that is, I had simply stopped fighting. I had stopped dreaming about being a warrior for change and decided to take the path of least resistance. I had stopped being a chingona.

I don't even remember why I was in the counselor's office in the first place. Maybe she had scheduled the appointment solely to appease her shock and curiosity. What I do remember was her cynical and derisive tone toward the end of her monologue. It became clear to me that I was supposed to be like the furniture in her office: a silent witness to her as she processed her own ideas and thoughts about my academic success out loud. Before I could even begin to formulate an answer, she blurted out, "I mean, if we could somehow bottle up your achievements, you know? Create a pill that allows others to do this? We could sell it and be rich!"

She stared at me, smiling brightly. I stared at her blankly, unsure of whether she intended that comment as a joke. Then I quickly forced out a single laugh-snort to diffuse the awkwardness. In reality, though, I was not amused. She treated me like a commodity, a curiosity. She was in shock that an "at-risk" kid could defy expectations.

I left contemplating her response more than the question. In some ways I was just as confused as the counselor about what had changed. All I knew was that I no longer had the fight in me, the chola spirit. Still, what was the big deal? As a

teenager who had started to seek validation through her studies, I thought it was a bit ridiculous to be *that* excited about
this change. Or was it?

Although I did not have an answer for her then, I now understand her response: change is hard, and the counselor wasn't
prepared to see it. She assumed that the path of least resistance
for me would have been to continue earning "bad" grades and
flunk out. I was, after all, the first in my family to go to high
school, and in two years I would become a first-generation
high school graduate. But for me the path of least resistance
was actually going along with the expectations of a star student.

Why would anyone purposefully seek uncharted waters and
go against expectations? Defy the acceptance of others? And
yet that is exactly what chingonas do: they transcend expectations. By doing so, they change the world around them. They
see beyond the dreams others have for them, and they dream
for themselves.

My counselor's question, my change, and her response to it stayed
with me for a long time. Was my academic turnaround truly a
miracle, or had I somehow created it purposefully? Was it something that happened *to* me or something I made happen? I know
now I was starting to understand my own agency in a system that
all too easily wants us to forget it. Though I had no answer for

her that day—and, like I said, I don't think she actually wanted one—I go back to this question in my mind from time to time. Why and how was I choosing this other path? What did it really mean? Why was it greeted so excitedly, almost like I had been "cured" of the rebellious disobedience I had exhibited prior? When I finally complied, it was applauded as the pinnacle of my teen life—a sign that I was ready to audition for the American dream of status and wealth. I was an "at-risk" kid who had gotten it together. No one seemed to be giving any thought to the educational system and what it was doing to people like me.

In other words, I had gone from resisting and fighting the system and to allowing myself to submit to it—to comply with the status quo and powers that be. Previously I had toyed with becoming a chola, which is what many people expected of an "at-risk" Chicana girl with no high school graduates in her family. Now I was simply allowing myself to take part in the flip side of those expectations: social control and the ubiquitous organization of our capitalist society. The opposite end of the binary meant going to school, studying, doing well, getting a "good" job, getting married, and having kids. Then I'd be ready to take part of the next set of expectations. My classmates and I were part of what Dr. Bettina Love, in her book *We Want to Do More Than Survive*, calls the "educational survival complex": educational institutions in America's history and present that are "overrun with dark suffering." In these educational systems, students are left "learning to merely survive, learning how schools mimic the world they live in, thus making schools a training site for a life of exhaustion." So I got in line with the expectations society had for me, for us all.

Everything within me resisted this conformity. In some ways, both scenarios—flunking out of high school (as the counselor had clearly been expected I would do) and succeeding academically and becoming a good girl (as I was now doing)—were paths of conformity, or paths of least resistance. Both paths produced accolades and rewards, just from different people. Both were expected routes to the future. Neither held space for truly transformative or countercultural change.

Questioning rules, social norms, and values in school and society would soon become a necessary part of my chingona journey. Neither dropping out nor garnering academic awards allowed me to question.

None of this was clear to me then, of course—all I knew is that the counselor's "get rich quick" joke fell flat for me. But I was awakening to the power within me to change and imagine and create new realities around me. I wonder how often others have this type of awakening. Is it possible to be fully aware of society's expectations—that you either fail or succeed in ways that they define—and still strive for a different world?

NAMING THE SEAMS

Even as my grades improved, I felt the pressure to go along, to not question anything. And I was rewarded for it. It was comfortable and safe. Unfortunately, I also drank the Kool-Aid of capitalism. Looking back, I know that this is how I lost myself along the way, why I could not recognize myself before that interview in my hotel room. Now able to participate in educational systems that spit out compliant citizens, I would soon be confusing the grind for the hustle, the system for my purpose. I became complicit even when there were obvious signs that the system and power structure I was partaking in had not been built with people like me in mind.

I am not simply talking about the way we are all constantly being socialized, but also what we are being socialized *into*. The pulse of what bell hooks calls "white supremacist capitalist patriarchy"—the giant-ass, not-so-hidden curriculum that depends on us getting in line with a colonial mentality—allows us to continue in generational cycles of apathy, of violence against others and ourselves at the expense of wholeness and well-being. It is straight-up toxic and unsustainable. When you give into that—the apathy, the lack of actually feeling fulfilled even as you're surrounded by all of what we would call "success"—you are complicit with society's expectations of you.

Owning your inner chingona means being unruly enough to question the status quo. But it is hard to balance the struggle of wanting to change the status quo while living inside of it. We all need to survive and make ends meet; how do we do that while resisting the very systems in which we are complicit? It takes intentional, subversive activity to work within an oppressive system.

Being part of something you don't fully believe in can bring up a lot of hopelessness and helplessness. That's how I felt in educational systems like high school and beyond. It is so easy to see ourselves as the problem in those instances. For a long time, I thought there was something wrong with *me*. How was I able to notice the stuff seeping out the seams of the world—educational injustice, racism, patriarchy, those toxic generational cycles of exhaustion—when many others simply and seemingly happily took part in these systems?

Unfortunately for my old counselor, change is definitely not something we can turn into a pill to bottle up and profit from. Indeed, my true change that year wasn't even an idea she might agree with or one she was hoping to hear. Yes, I had begun caring about my classes and enjoying learning and finding a sense of accomplishment as I applied myself. But what I had truly tapped into that year, besides my own agency, was subversive activity: the antidote to the path of least resistance.

Even while my grades were going up, I was also beginning to question why, in history classes, everything revolved around wealthy white men. In English classes, I was asking questions about who wrote, published, and sold the books. In biology, I was wondering how the divine played into the seemingly calculated, beautiful chaos of the universe, and whether microbiological patterns could not be seen as divine in and of themselves. I was putting the chola in scholar. Seeing the perplexed expressions of authority figures in response to my questions— their "I don't get paid enough to do this" faces—breathed power and hope back into my own life. After all, I had blamed myself for the hopelessness and helplessness for so long.

Then there were the times I was called out for my subversive behavior or probing questions—getting called a "socialist," "idealist," or "anarchist," for instance. Change is hard. And though it stung when I was perceived as the problem because I was calling out the *actual* problem—in what was not considered history, for example, or in binary ways of thinking that dominated the curriculum—I hold these memories as badges of honor. Those were my true As: my good grades in subversive activity as I worked within the system.

I didn't yet have the language for it, but now I can see that I was learning about the borderlands, the in-between spaces, the land of the unknown. I felt stuck, and I thought I needed a way out of the in-betweenness. But what I actually needed was a way to go deeper into the in-betweenness. I didn't need a way out of the borderlands; I needed a way *in*.

NEPANTLA

I'm grateful to have discovered the work of Gloria Anzaldúa, a Chicana theorist who gives us the feminist language of nepantla: liminal lands and spaces. This is terrain many chingonas have come to occupy. Frequently, chingonas are those who live in nepantla—in the middle—and we've lived in the borderlands for so long that it has become part of our identity. We are ni de aqui, ni de alla, in the words of Anzaldúa: not from here, nor from there.

In reality, Anzaldúa was the one who made the concept of nepantla accessible; our common ancestors actually gave us this language. Nepantla is a Nahuatl term used by the Aztecs to describe a space in the middle or in between. "Transformations occur in this in-between space, an unstable, unpredictable, precarious, always-in-transition space lacking clear boundaries," Anzaldúa writes. "Nepantla es tierra desconocida, and living in this liminal zone means being in a constant state of displacement—an uncomfortable, even alarming feeling."

We often try to fix all that is unresolved within us, to defy that uncomfortable, alarming feeling of in-betweenness. But as nepantleras—border crossers and dwellers—chingonas have to deal with this temptation to resolve the contradictions of life. We have to learn to rest and live in that complexity. We have to allow all the parts within us to integrate, to heal, and we have to learn to live in the wholeness and richness of the in-between spaces.

Before I was able to own my identity as a chingona, I needed to simply let myself be. I needed to learn to rest in the identity of nepantlera. Crossing borders and living in in-between spaces is a necessary part of the chingona journey.

Later I would discover another ancient concept that would help me make sense of chingona identity. The Aztecs believed that living is an exercise in balance. Living means facing continuous harsh interruptions, they believed, and just as the earth itself is always changing, life was understood as always in flux and unpredictable. Life, both the physical and spiritual, is change. The Aztecs understood earth, and life itself, as slick and slippery: unpredictable, ever-changing and in flux, and unable to be controlled. Some scholars suggest that this belief strongly influenced the Nahua people as "way-seeking" rather than "truth-seeking." They valued guidance and wisdom that led to rootedness and balance over doctrines or assertions of truth. Finding rootedness and balance in Teotl (the life force) was a high virtue in Aztec communities.

For Aztecs, discernment grows when you develop what Miguel Leon-Portilla translates as a "wise face and good heart."

They believed that the face (as part of the head) is where growth and development resides in the human body, and that the heart is where knowledge and wisdom comes to life. In college and graduate school, however, I was not yet ready to develop a "wise face and good heart." Finding rootedness and balance is difficult in your young adult years, especially if stopping to consider your actions and beliefs triggers an impending sense of doom, as it did for me. Getting stuck forever in an in-between place can make a person really uncomfortable, and that is exactly what it felt like for me to stop and discern as a young adult. It was easier to keep moving.

During my college years, I was busy chasing desires, sometimes seemingly altruistic ones, but nevertheless I was driven by them. Overworking, even for a good cause, and being driven by achievement are addictive drugs. When I had minor setbacks, I used dating to pick me back up, and I definitely lacked judgment there. (I mean, I *was* in my twenties, and I feel like everyone who was ever twenty deserves a pass here.) Even now, it is still hard sometimes to not chase a shiny new accomplishment. If I do not stop to align my head with my heart and discern my desires, I go to the easiest and fastest next thing I need to feel fulfilled. In those years of study, I was convinced that all my hard work would deliver me from the fear of stopping and judging my life's meaning. I didn't want to have to discern a way forward, and I had no idea what it would look like to live rooted. I only knew what it was like to fall on this slick and slippery existence of life. But perhaps stopping to discern is what midlife is all about.

Awakening to the conveyor belts, learning to live in nepantla territory, and finding rootedness—these are difficult tasks. Nepantla territory is scary and lonely, but beginning to dwell within it also taught me about resistance and courage. I could resist the status quo, which included both others' expectations of who I would become and my own fear about having to choose a way.

Moving into my master's and doctoral work, I was an outsider. I personified a way of living and contributed ideas that challenged the system itself, and I realized that some of my colleagues and professors viewed my mere presence in the academy as foreboding. In higher education, as in so many other fields and institutions, there has been generational resistance to my way of knowing. Latinas make up only about 4 percent of full-time professors in the United States, and that number was a lot lower not that long ago.

Living in nepantla, in the in-betweenness, requires work. Ironically, taking moments to pause and discern next steps requires work. Sometimes resting can make chingonas feel like time is wasting away—like we are running late or falling behind.

But times of reflection can be intentional and active; purpose can be found in the waiting. Moments of pause allow us to practice rootedness, too. In them we can find balance between doing and being, and we can reflect on our priorities and values. I often feel like I should be doing something in those moments of rest. It is hard to find contentment that way. The thing about finding something external to help you feel whole is that the pursuit is never ending and always elusive. The moment after you receive that external affirmation, you already feel defeated—because you know you'll need more to feel okay again.

Owning your inner chingona means learning to pause. Rest can prevent you from constantly falling on this "slick and slippery" earth and life. Finding time to rest can allow you to realize how you are leading and contributing, creating change in yourself or in others around you.

CULTURAL COYOTES

Chingonas understand the gift it is to be on new and complex paths. We have the courage required to show up and keep fighting. It is the chola-within-the-scholar spirit we carry. Pausing to reflect on the in-betweenness teaches us about the power in marginal spaces. And it makes us yearn to share what we've learned with others.

Being part of a community is important to chingonas, too. We share power with others because we desire that our gente be able to enter all the new spaces we have entered. For me, my people include my family but also my ethnic and ancestral community.

When I finally stopped to rest and discern, years after I completed my doctoral studies, I realized that I had a platform for sharing with others wisdom about resisting internalized colonialism and learning about nepantlera identity. Although my audience wasn't huge and my impact wasn't far reaching, through a podcast I cohost and a collective on trauma and healing that I founded, I was having important and often public conversations about social justice, race, and faith. In so doing, I was creating change and making space for others who also feel at odds because their voices are not represented in major outlets. Pausing to reflect was how I realized I had worked hard and long toward a career as an equity-minded educator and empowered others along the way. I realized I was supporting others in their own struggles of in-betweenness, in the exciting and scary new places they were forging.

Being the first in my family to graduate from high school and college was about forging my own path, but I wanted to bring my whole family and my community along. As my career has progressed, I have entered new emotional, intellectual, spiritual, social, political, cultural, and physical lands. Walking onto stages and into boardrooms, churches, and other spaces, I often felt like they were not meant for us, for my gente. But I wanted my gente next to me.

I was and am a cultural coyote: someone who travels between lands and carries others with them into new spaces. A coyote helps others bridge unknown lands. A coyote's job is to help people cross borders. They help frightened people navigate and find their way across deserts, streams, and mountains, helping them read signs in nature to navigate their way to new lands. Although coyotes have gotten a bad rap because some exploit vulnerable migrants with high prices and working with cartels, the trusted coyote from someone's community is still the safest bet. We who live between worlds can help others make their way into these spaces too. Bringing my family and others in my community to the proverbial table that had been kept from us, I had begun building a different table altogether—a more inclusive, caring, and tolerant one. We can no longer wait to be invited to the table. We are building our own.

In this way, when we operate as cultural coyotes, we carry a certain amount of power. Chingonas acknowledge the way we, too, can perpetuate abusive leadership styles and controlling power. This type of power cost my ancestors their way of living, their dreams, the honoring of the way-seeking paths they were on.

In order to acknowledge the cost of abusive leadership and controlling power, I needed to admit to myself that I was waiting for an apology from white people—those I saw as the colonizers of mi gente. But after no apologies came, I realized that what I truly desired was intergenerational healing and shared power. I resented the fact that my community lived in survival mode due to the violence and dehumanization that colonization brought. I knew that unless something changed, future generations would continue in this colonial mindset, which would prevent them from experiencing true psychic freedom from pain. This realization—that I desired an apology that would not come—is nepantla territory for certain. When we long for change that is not assured, we are living in the in-betweenness.

I had to balance my desire for healing with my longing for judgment. I had to develop a "wise face and good heart," as the Aztecs teach, and recognize that while an apology would not come from others, I can still find inner balance and peace. This acceptance is not a passive dismissal of the generational hurt due to abuse in power: it is an active patience of living in the in-between.

SEEING OURSELVES AS LEADERS

The reality is that we have to learn and relearn all these lessons over and over again. Over the last years, I have dedicated my professional life to supporting the educational aspirations of first-generation college students from working-class backgrounds. At a recent professional development event for the nonprofit I work for, a guest speaker led us in an activity in which we had to come up with examples of leaders.

My group was composed of mostly first-generation college graduates and professionals. Two people in my group were in leadership positions within our organization, serving as directors, and I was very interested in what they would share. We were all people of color, mainly from Latine backgrounds. After we completed the activity, we were to share with the group at large. When it was time to share, my group's answer to the question about who we saw as leaders included a range of people: from widely known heroes of the past to family members who had showed courage and leadership by immigrating to a new country.

A break followed—and, as with many such events, that is when the real, unscripted conversations began. We began to realize that none of us had named any of the leaders from *within* our group as models. Clearly we had good examples of leadership within our group! So why hadn't we mentioned any? Curious and confused, we wondered aloud why colleagues who were in leadership positions in the organization didn't see themselves as leaders. They were minimizing their roles and expertise. One colleague, who aspires to become a manager someday, was brought to tears as she recalled a time a boss told her she could not be a leader.

I looked around at my coworkers. There was a single mom of a teen; she had been hustling for so long, busy chasing success, that she simply hadn't considered that she might be a leader. But she definitely was. Another woman—one in a director role, who had experience working in settings across the nation—also didn't see herself as a leader. I started naming the people in my group who were leaders, wondering aloud why they didn't see themselves as leaders. Just then someone in our group looked straight at me and said with a bit of exasperation, "Alma, you are a leader too!"

The comment stopped me short. There I was, the only one in the room with a PhD, a large following on social media, and a popular podcast. Degrees and social media followings and podcasts don't automatically make you a leader, of course, but they suggest a level of authority that I hadn't been prepared to see. I was singing the praises of those I thought were the "real" leaders in the room, wondering why they didn't identify as leaders, but I hadn't even thought to ask myself the same question.

Was I a leader? *Am* I a leader? If so, when had that transition happened? Had we all been too busy to notice our impact and influence on our families, colleagues, younger people, and communities? Too busy to integrate all of who we were—not just our achievements and hard work but also a grounding confidence in ourselves? When did we lose sight of ourselves as leaders? Or why had we never claimed that identity in the first place?

This is part and parcel of how colonialism works: by getting into the minds and imaginations of people of color and colonizing our views of ourselves and what is possible. At some point, many of us lose the imagination necessary to see ourselves as leaders. We miss the fact that somewhere along the way, in the words of Alice Walker, we have become "the ones we have been waiting for."

CULTURAL COYOTE LEADERSHIP

As I sat across from my colleagues—scratch that: from other *leaders*—at the professional development luncheon at work that day, I began to wonder if we couldn't see ourselves as leaders because we had let others—people who do not know us—tell us what a leader is, what a leader looks like, and how to be one.

Leaders come in all shapes and sizes and with different backgrounds and experiences. Sure, we can bemoan the fact that others were given access or finances or the "right" skin color. We may look at our past and think, "I don't have the right education, opportunities, family, or connections." Then we convince ourselves that we are not cut out for the job. We see certain representations of leaders on TV: people who are larger than life, confident, often white and male, and who always seem to say the right things and wear the right clothes. But those things do not make one a leader. We can complain that we do not have big enough influence and impact, that we have no mentors. But maybe we just haven't had the eyes to see those who showed up as mentors and guides in our lives—the cultural coyotes who came before us. Perhaps some of them helped us across the unknown terrain, and perhaps we have simply forgotten about them.

We who are cultural coyotes bring our people along with us into new spaces and new roles, and we have so much to balance as we bridge new paths and identities. In the process, we sometimes lose sight of ourselves, our rootedness. We don't take time for depth and vulnerability with one another. We replace the calling with the grind.

Leaders are everyday people balancing discernment and desire. Cultural coyote leadership will look a lot different from the styles of leadership we'd learned in school. Cultural coyote leadership is about healing and mending. Somewhere along the way we came to believe in a very narrow view of who a leader is and what the journey to leadership looks like, and we believed that we were not meant to lead.

Becoming a leader is about more than being a survivor living in the in-betweenness. True leadership of the cultural coyote variety makes in-betweenness the point. Cultural coyote leaders lead from a place of discomfort and hope. We make the lostness the lesson, the deep place from where we lead.

Leadership isn't always about a big, shiny fancy stage. It is about compassion, humility, and resilience. It is about the role of our communities, never being alone in our lostness, and bringing everyone along to rejoice in it with us.

We also have to be ready for "the slick and slippery" earth, as the Aztecs said—the unknown changes we will face in life. Leadership requires rootedness. I learned more about rootedness during graduate school, in what I had previously thought was a greedy white man's religion. I had thought of Christianity as a faith of the colonizers—the spiritual structure that justified the taking of land and religion and other people's bodies.

Except when I looked closer, I realized that the Christian faith didn't need to be greedy or white or just for men. This faith tradition was a rootedness available for all. It was born from a group of people fighting power from the margins, and from a man, Jesús, who crossed borders and lived in in-between spaces. This faith has become a spiritual path that helps me understand the lostness we sometimes feel in the in-betweenness. It illuminates the allure and deception of the conveyor belts. It calls out those hoarding power, and it honors a different type of leadership, one where the least in our communities are put first. It helps me learn to lead from a place of marginality. When I can no longer keep up with the lucha, I remember my ancestor, Jesús, and how he defied it all—the whole freaking system. He was the original mentor in having a "wise face and good heart."

When we own our inner chingona, we can claim the potential to change within ourselves, families, communities, and histories. Leadership is about healing and mending in nepantla territory. Healing and growth are leadership work, because when we confront the colonial order, we begin to relax the muscles of our possible futures. When we heal, we use trauma and trade it for resilience. We lean into vulnerability and honesty. We own the complexity of complicity. We find contentment.

6

FROM PUSHED OUT TO MIJANESS

Reenvision Your Identity

I find I am constantly being encouraged to pluck out some one aspect of myself and present this as the meaningful whole, eclipsing or denying the other parts of self.

—AUDRE LORDE

n the fall of 2016, when Donald Trump was elected president, I was teaching at a small private liberals arts college. I had recently graduated from my doctoral program, and I had been trying to make sense of all the parts of me—parts that felt dissociated from one another. How did I come to be a radical feminist Mexicana and also an educator in a system designed to keep people like me out? How had I come to be someone who wants to heal personally and also wants to live in a more socially just world? Someone who both loves Jesus *and* digs deep into ancestral spirituality? These identities seemed so contradictory, so oxymoronic.

One thing was certain, though: for a long time I had felt pushed out of life, excluded from spaces designed for others. I had joined a doctoral department that had pushed out five other Latina students before I even arrived. Some of the pushed-out students had even tried to warn me about the political climate in the department before I began my studies. By the time I completed my dissertation, even the faculty women of color had left.

So in the fall of 2016, I had stepped in to teach a class on privilege and oppression called The Social Construction of Difference. As Trump won and white supremacist and extremist groups were emboldened, many people like me—women of color, children of immigrants—felt completely unwelcome in this country. Brown women have a long history with conquerors, and it looked like we would just have to hold on for the ride.

That fall, during one of our very first classes, a young white male student asked a question. Why did we even have to understand the oppressed, he asked, when they were just people who didn't know how to win? Clearly they had been on the losing side of history. Why couldn't we instead recognize the winners for being smarter and stronger than the others? What he didn't say but was clear by his rhetoric and his tone was this: the experiences of the oppressed didn't matter to him. We were not worth listening to or learning from.

The student's question was a harsh introduction to what teaching would look like for me that year—an uphill battle to help students understand the unintended and intended consequences of greed, power, and colonization. Luckily, as the professor, I didn't have to respond. Several chingona students in the class immediately began asking him questions and poking holes that let some light into that young man's dark logic.

How hard is it to stay curious when you've been fighting so hard to simply be allowed to exist? How difficult is it to heal and grow when you've simply been trying to survive? That student's question was a clear indication of the work that I would have to do: to stay curious, to heal, to remain human in a dehumanizing system, and to claim my identities, even my contradictory ones.

Being a chingona means reenvisioning your identity and doing so in contexts that do not welcome your complexity or contradictions. It means being able to hold on to the contradictions of who—and why—you are. As you deal with new struggles and challenges, you don't need to be held back by your old roles and identities or the way others once perceived you. As you begin to own your inner chingona, you awaken to the role of your past and to how even painful memories give you space to root deeper into your true identity.

I have my own contradictions, and perhaps you do too. On the one hand, I have a Catholic upbringing that included colonial Christian beliefs; on the other, I have a faith rooted in social justice and ancestral spirituality. On the one hand, I am an educator committed to liberatory learning like Paulo Freire outlined in *Pedagogy of the Oppressed*; on the other, I sometimes teach in oppressive systems that still dehumanize people of color and people from working-class backgrounds. As the daughter of immigrants, I also hold the contradiction of both looking for a better way of life in this country and feeling anger toward its xenophobic political leaders.

Coming to terms with our contradictions—and doing so within our contexts, which are not necessarily conducive to our growth—requires us to imagine beyond them. We need to find a new language for our unique and complicated experiences. Digging deeply into my own identity has been a scary journey, but I know that is exactly why I need to do it. In the process of owning my inner chingona, I have heard a gentle invitation: to love myself, my curiosity, and my creativity.

Growing up, I was always struck by the image of the Aztec warrior carrying the princess. The legend of Popocatepetl and Iztaccíhuatl's love story has been used to explain the origin of two of the largest volcanoes in the Western Hemisphere, which tower above Mexico City. One of the volcanoes looks like a woman lying on her back, and the other like a man crouching next to her. There are various versions of the story in Mexican folklore, but essentially the princess, Iztaccíhuatl, dies of a broken heart believing that her lover, Popocatepetl, has died in battle. Upon his return from battle, the warrior learns of Iztaccíhuatl's death and, in grief, carries her to a mountain range. There they stay together eternally, covered in snow.

I can't usually relate to the woman being carried, and I don't like to imagine myself as weak, faint, or dead. So I have often imagined myself to be the warrior. But as I come to terms with my own contradictions and growth, I realize that I am both the Aztec warrior carrying the princess *and* the princess needing to be carried. Loving your full self is about reimagining yourself and the learning from the experiences that have caused you pain and heartache. Reenvisioning your identity is what being a chingona is all about.

As you keep reimagining yourself, you have to find the ganas to fight for your identity. *Ganas*: I love this word. It evokes both winning *and* having the will or the desire. You have to want to win in order to even have a shot at doing so. *Echale ganas*: give it your all, try as hard as you can. Ganas is about courage.

Chingona courage is what my students had that day as they challenged their peer who could not see beyond his own logic. You have to find the ganas to imagine how your contradictory identities can hold together. You need ganas to venture into new lands—both physical terrain and lands of imagination and possibility to which our ancestors were denied. You can enter wholeness via somatic and mystical landscapes—lands where we are a part of each other.

A RAINBOW VISION

I was completing a hike between rain showers when I first heard the news that Joe Biden had formally been declared the winner of the 2020 presidential election. I had been anticipating the announcement for a couple days, and I was feeling anxious on and off all week as results from key states rolled in. "Ganó, ganó, ganó!" had been the exuberant if somewhat premature llanto of my neighbor earlier in the week, when it began to look as if Joe Biden had won. The only other time I had heard such joyful screams coming from my neighbors' home was when the Los Angeles Dodgers became the World Series champions after three long decades.

Like my neighbor, I, too, had worried about what it would mean to live under four more years of a Trump presidency. But in those days between the election and the official announcement of Biden's win, I almost didn't dare hope for something different.

Earlier that November day, after waiting out the rain, checking the weather predictions, and pulling out of my driveway to go to my usual hiking spot, I had been greeted by the clearest and biggest rainbow I had seen in years splayed majestically over all of Boyle Heights. That rainbow was beautiful and grounding, and even though I hadn't yet heard the news of Trump's defeat, I couldn't help but feel that the rainbow was for us: for me and mi gente.

When I saw that rainbow and as I drove out to the hiking trail, I reflected on *The Red Couch Podcast*, which my partner and I had launched as a direct response to Trump's ascension to the highest public office in 2016. Back then, many people suddenly felt displaced—pushed out of their own faith communities and families, hurt by the conflation of nationalism with their faith—and were looking for alternative spaces. They wanted to make sense of what it meant to be Christian in the United States when so many other Christians had supported Trump. We hoped to be a voice for marginalized communities in faith and spiritual spaces. We were motivated to start the podcast by our love for those who found themselves displaced from faith spaces and their families.

That day, in the waiting period after the election but before the announcement of final results, I could not help but think of my years as a doctoral student and how hard that season had been, both because I was going through so many personal changes and also because of the racial aggressions and white supremacist practices I experienced. I recalled how excluded and unwelcome I felt in that department, in society, and even in my own skin. After my doctoral studies were complete, the adrenaline from the fight response I had allowed my body to exist in for so long had diminished. As I moved away from survival mode, my mind and body gave in, and I needed to reconcile to myself, my spirit. I had done very little to stay grounded and rooted through the whirlwind of those years.

Some chaos had occurred in my personal life during Trump's residency in the White House. I had been married for a little over a year and had become a practicing Protestant—having been raised Catholic—just a year prior to that. During our first years of marriage and my time in graduate school, I found myself in mostly conservative and predominantly white churches. Although I loved the church we attended because it helped me rediscover my faith and offered me what I thought, at the time, was "sound" theology, these were hard years as I balanced being a mother, a wife to a traveling artist, and a full-time student. I felt misunderstood and unknown at both the church and the university I attended.

I had told myself I would figure out these disparate parts of me *after* I was done with my doctoral studies. Someday, I told myself, I'd resolve the contradictions within myself. This was the same attitude I held about my role as a partner in marriage during those years—though of course it doesn't work that way. So soon after graduating, I had to pick up the pieces of my newfound faith, identity, and marriage, and finally give them the time they deserved. This was painstaking work but very much needed. It felt like the beginning of a new life, a rebirth.

On the hike that day, I was reminded, too, of hope, love, and resilience through pain and struggle. It had been a long year. I had started writing this book in February 2019, weeks before a worldwide pandemic hit that meant so many people would lose jobs, homes, and lives. A few months into our quarantined life, George Floyd was murdered by a police officer, and a racial uprising broke out all over the nation. The uprising was long overdue and had been years in the making. Many people were weighing not only the effects of trauma upon a nation but also upon individuals. No doubt, the racial reckoning that occurred in 2020 was a result of ongoing efforts by people of color and a shifting global consciousness.

For years now I had been searching for a spiritual understanding of our connectedness and communal purpose. To understand how my personal experience was connected to the holy, I had to reenvision my own spiritual identity.

INCENSE, SOCIAL JUSTICE, AND THE HOLY

Reenvisioning our identities means understanding our uniqueness and holding on to the contradictions this understanding might expose. Owning our inner chingona means understanding both that we are a product of our contexts *and* that we have agency. Yes, we are shaped by how we were raised, but we also make choices that shape our selves.

One of the forces that shapes many of us, and many of our contradictions, is religion. Growing up, I was as devout a Catholic as first-generation Mexican Americans come. I went through all my sacraments and quinceañera ceremony through the Catholic Church.

Now I see the ways in which adults used religion to keep us as kids and young adults in line. Faith became a parenting tool to threaten us into obedience, at times operating much like la chancla. But instead of the threat of beating you with a shoe, religion gave us threats of a fiery hell. This instilled a fear of the future and what awaited me after death. Fear is what kept me obedient and practicing the faith. I was taught about a judging, wrathful, and vengeful God, who is exclusionary and unwelcoming. I didn't hear much about a caring, loving, and gentle God, and I didn't experience that type of love outside of Mass much either. I imagine that is why it has been hard to for me to be gentle, steady, and loving with myself. Imagining God as a patient gardener who tends to my soul—which is how I now view God—was difficult or even impossible.

But here's the contradiction: this same faith taught me about social justice. In fact, the Catholic Church was where my love for social justice first got ignited. It was in la iglesia that I first heard stories of helping others through community and social change. Dismantling power and privilege and loving one another were common themes in Mass. The Spanish-speaking and bilingual priests talked about imigración, politics, and getting along. They taught us to see beyond nationality and finances and instead to treat ourselves and each other as part of a bigger family.

Catholicism was the only place that I ever heard truths and philosophies that resonated with my lived experience. We helped others through our donations and by attending the latest kermeses, festival-like gatherings to raise funds for the needs of particular families. It was also in Mass that I first heard of ideals of unity, love, and forgiveness. Church presented a reality beyond my immediate surroundings, my family, the news, and the hood. This gave me hope, hope that people could care for others beyond their immediate families, beyond even their own cultural communities.

In Mass, my belief in the immaterial solidified. The padres were the first visionaries I met, and they made me believe there was more to life than the physical body and concrete experiences. Observing the entrance procession and watching how the smoke from the incense seemed to dance throughout the room connected me to the sacred. The liturgy of Mass—the kneeling, standing, kissing, bowing, and striking of our chests in unison—felt holy, and it brought me joy. My thoughts would drift into the air as I thought about what all this meant. Why were we all alive together in this moment? Why did we have separate consciousnesses? And how close were our consciousnesses to God's plan? How unified and connected were we with the divine and each other?

Almost as if they could sense the questions filling my mind, my parents would elbow me to continue chanting scripture when they noticed I was now longer really there, no longer paying attention. I would join and rejoin scripture chanting again and again throughout Mass, elbow dig after elbow dig, giving myself golpes for being a sinner even though I did not understand what this meant.

Still, thoughts about La Virgencita, the mother of Jesus—her sadness and transcendent love for the oppressed—filled my soul. She was so familiar. Her beautiful brown skin and intense dark eyes were just like those of my mother and abuelita and tias and other women in my family. Her divinity was intimately personal. The image of her indigenous roots was even more so: Tonantzin, Our Sacred Mother.

In those early years I was not yet questioning religion or deconstructing my faith. I wasn't yet skeptical about the immaterial world, and it didn't bother me that I couldn't understand or explain what was happening around me. I was mostly in love with the mystery of faith, and I was okay with no answers. I was satisfied with my personal experience with Our Sacred Mother.

As I looked across the pews and saw the faith and holiness of it all—the hope in a God who would redeem and save—I was fascinated. How could such very different people come together and believe in something they could not see? How could they know they were right in picking this religion, this particular way of encountering the divine?

It wasn't until much later that I realized most of us are born into these belief systems. In my late teens I stopped believing in the magic place that the liturgy used to take me to. The inconsistencies I saw—between the words and actions of people in the church—overwhelmed me. I couldn't reconcile how people could both love and feel loved by God and yet treat others with hate and exclude them. I blamed God for that.

I became curious about other belief systems, so I explored many. Across all spiritualities and religions, I saw that people were practicing things in the contexts they had inherited. They simply believed what their families believed, and they simply listened to the interpreters of their spiritual knowledge and teachings. In Western Catholicism, only men were allowed to be clergy members, and I began to realize that this was why, as a kid, I had to confess mis pecados to a grown man. When I became an evangelical Christian, I attended a church that offered theology from a white, male, Eurocentric perspective. As I studied other religions and looked more critically at my own, I realized that I couldn't blame God for all of this. It was us, people, who were creating these conditions and oppressive systems.

Deconstruction has become a buzzword in Western Christian circles, especially as many white evangelicals openly embraced nationalism and racism and xenophobia in their support of Donald Trump. Many people of color and those who believe in an inclusive God have, as a result, questioned what churches claim to be correct theology. Being without a faith home and community can be a scary place to be. But this arrebato, this daze, is necessary for growth and healing.

MIJA SPIRITUALITY

That November day, as I saw my rainbow vision and hiked through foothills between rain showers, I kept remembering the padres, the Mass, and my social justice ideals. I thought, too, about the nation and Western Christian churches, and how they seemed a little less hypocritical that day. I was being too optimistic, perhaps, to think that white Christian nationalism would not again rear its head in the coming years. But for that moment, I was glad that one evil had been made a little lesser, a little less dominant. The United States, like myself, is broken from the effects of trauma. Tending to the spiritual wounding and brokenness was part of my journey toward self-discovery and healing, and I was giving myself space to root deeper into my own chingona journey. I hoped my country could do the same.

The compounding trauma I had experienced as a child and young adult had manifested as depression and anxiety and harmful coping mechanisms. Despite the many experiences I had as a child, though, for many years I did not let go of wonder. For a long time I held on to a sense of excitement about what could be and what was in store. But as years went on and I continued to fight without rest, I had lost that wonder. It is hard to ground and root yourself in truths when you have no grounding to come "home" to anymore. When we keep imagining and reimagining ourselves from a hate-, fear-, or shame-filled place, we get nowhere. But when we reenvision ourselves from a God-within-me source, we grow.

Healing from trauma, accepting our contradictions, and envisioning a just and healed world—these all require healing from a true curandero. On that hike, I felt a strong sense that I was reclaiming my authentic mijaness—"daughterness," you could call it—through my healer, Jesus. This identity as mija goes beyond good and evil, which were the categories of both my Catholic childhood and evangelical adulthood. Mija spirituality encompasses the ancient wisdom of my Mesoamerican Indigenous people, as well as my spiritual encounter with Jesus and La Virgencita. Sometimes I think about my grandmother's shrine to La Virgencita—to Tonantzin—and the way she lovingly tended to it. I remember that I am the daughter—the mija—of all these ancestors. Mija spirituality is about being la hija rebelde, and about putting back together Coyolxauhqui. I have felt the rootedness of reawakening to mindbodyspirit well-being. I've come back home to the mystery of the divine that always lived within me.

Owning our inner chingona means growing and growing and growing some more. Sometimes we discover we need new skin because we have outgrown the old, like the wise and precious feathered serpent, Quetzalcoatl, an Aztec deity. In the K'iche' Mayan account of creation, the gods Hurakan and Gugumatz are analogous to Quetzalcoatl. Quetzalcoatl symbolizes fertility, renewal, and transformation. As it sheds its own skin, it becomes new.

As we move from one vessel to another, we are transformed and renewed. We shed the old, worn-out layers and expand into wider vessels that have more room for all parts of ourselves. We propagate our own spirit. We move from a seedling to a bud to a flowering and ripening sacred temple that feeds many.

Corporations and governments and religions can try to objectify, commodify, and sell you this process of personal growth and spiritual transformation. They can try to simplify and predict it. Yet try as they may, systems cannot produce true spiritual liberation. As you grow into your inner chingona, you must dig deep into your own contradictions to own your spiritual identity. Mija spirituality fills a mother wound and rebeldia consciousness for me. It reminds me of the precolonial way of my ancestors.

COYOTE VISION

On my hike that November day, I ran into a couple of coyotes. Coyotes hold strong symbolism in many Native American tribes, and the word *coyote* itself is from a Nahuatl word, coyōtl, which means "trickster." The Aztecs believed in Huēhuecoyōtl, or Very Old Trickster, which is the god of music, dance, mischief, and pleasure and is symbolized by the coyote. The coyote is considered cunning, resourceful, and adaptable. Like I was coming to understand about myself, the coyote is neither entirely evil nor entirely good. It is both, and it symbolizes balance. Many other Indigenous tribes ascribe to the coyote a similar wisdom and sense of humor. In myth and legend, coyotes are a reminder to not take life so seriously and to strive for balance instead.

This November day wasn't the first time I had run into coyotes on this trail. Years earlier I had almost come face to face with one of them as I followed a trail that wasn't well marked. Dense bushes and a narrowing path had me crouching lower and lower to keep on the trail until, after taking several steps in this way, I decided that this was no way to hike and got back onto the regular trail. When I stepped away and looked back, curious about where that side trail may have led had I continued on it, I saw a coyote, standing just a couple of feet ahead of me, on the trail I had just exited.

I locked eyes with the animal, and we both just stood there for a bit, watching each other. Surprisingly, I felt an overwhelming sense of calm and peace for a moment. Soon my rational mind

FROM PUSHED OUT TO MIJANESS

would start internally screaming, and I would realize how scary the situation was. Soon I would walk away as quickly as I could, and I would spend the rest of my hike terrified that I was being followed and that the coyote would be hiding in the bushes along the way. But for a moment, Huēhuecoyōtl looked at me, and I looked back.

Now, on my November 2016 hike, I remembered that earlier encounter, and I considered that perhaps the coyote had had a message for me. I thought back to the incense in la iglesia, how it had a message about the transcendent nature of life, the metaphysical, and I wondered what the coyote might be saying.

Not long after I began wondering about coyotes and balance and messages, I encountered two coyotes on the trail—separately but back to back, only about 100 feet away from each other. We literally crossed paths, as I was walking one way on the hiking trail and they were walking the other, opposite me, on the same trail. As I walked past one and then the other, I wondered whether I should run or hide or cry out for help. Except no one was around. Instead, I took my phone out and took pictures of them. I decided to document it all. If they wanted to attack me or suddenly decided to, I thought, well, I could not do much more about it at this point.

So that November weekend, as I remembered that time with the coyote years ago and as I took pictures of these two, I smiled. Perhaps this Very Old Trickster was reminding me I could have a sense of humor about all the contradictions in myself and in the contexts in which I live. Perhaps I could learn from him to be resourceful and adaptable. Perhaps there is wisdom in enjoying oneself despite—or in the middle of—the pain.

As I completed the hike that day, I checked the news on my phone and found out that Joe Biden and Kamala Harris had officially won the election. We had, for the first time ever, elected a woman of color, born of immigrant parents, to the vice presidency. This has been many lifetimes in the making.

Elated, I got into my car to drive back toward the city. Feeling something like a coyote, engrossed in my own trickery, humor, and mischief, I drove back to the city blasting YG's "F*** Donald Trump" song. Cathartic tears blended with crazed laughter as I pulled up in front of my favorite coffee shop. Honks filled the streets all around East Los Angeles, and people on the sidewalk were cheering, clapping, and hooting.

Sitting in my car, I read texts from Latina, Black, and white coconspirator friends reminding me of the importance of this moment for our girls, the ones we were raising and those around the nation. Chingonas have to stay curious and creative for the future. We have to remind each other of the possibilities. It is how we find the strength to reenvision our identities when we are dehumanized and pushed out politically and institutionally.

Looking back now, the rainbow that met me in the sky that morning as I left home for my hike seems supernatural, metaphysical. It felt on purpose, like a gentle and loving reminder that waiting for personal healing and social change sometimes starts to crystallize into something meaningful. It was a renewal, full of possibility.

7

VIVIR CON CICATRIZES

See Your Scars as Proof of Healing

I came to theory because I was hurting—the pain within me was so intense that I could not go on living. I came to theory desperate, wanting to comprehend— to grasp what was happening around and within me. Most importantly, I wanted to make the hurt go away. I saw theory then a location for healing.

—BELL HOOKS

Learning to live in peace, joy, and harmony with yourself and others is an important step in owning your inner chingona. But to do so, you need to understand your own woundedness. Understanding your own wounds is not a pleasant task, and it requires naming the forces and traumas that have acted upon your body, mind, and spirit.

We all carry a cicatriz, a scar, whether visible or invisible, on our bodies or minds or spirits. Understanding psychic wounds requires us to let go of the narratives that suggest we are only physical, logical beings. As we saw in earlier chapters, naming our wounds means journeying back into childhood, and sometimes beyond, to discover the source.

Many of us are products of a long story of oppression, and many of us have ancestors who were on both sides of the colonial project. This disharmony between our ancestors—this split identity—can lead to a rupture of the mindbodyspirit connection. So instead of joy and peace, we learn to practice fear and helplessness. Instead of harmony within ourselves, we feel the forces of history fighting each other in our bodies— and yes, we resort to the paradigm of war to describe what we experience! We don't truly understand our own body's inherent power and creativity to resist, survive, and thrive.

We often think of scars as evidence of wounds—and they are. But they are also proof of healing. Our bodies heal by forming scar tissue. In fact, medical professionals sometimes use the term *cicatrize* to describe the act of healing through the growth of scar tissue. Our wounds can cicatrize—be healed—through scarring.

So, chingonas stop and consider the scars rather than ignoring them. More importantly, we see cicatrizes as signs of healing, not just of pain. For me, therapy became a healing space where I was able to find a wound I had held for so many years. The wound was not physical; it was invisible, one that lived within my body. Healing is not linear; it's cyclical and beyond the rationality of the mind. It is a transcendent and spiritual process.

We need to stop seeing scars as only evidence of brokenness; we need to start seeing them as evidence of healing. I needed to let my spirit lead in the process of sanación, of healing. And as bell hooks writes, "I came to theory because I was hurting." When I wanted to understand my own psychic wounds and the intergenerational trauma that lived in my body, I began to theorize about my scars.

Owning your inner chingona involves learning mindbodyspirit awareness. Naming and reframing your scars. Trusting yourself to find harmony, joy, and peace.

What scars do you carry? How can you see them as signs of healing rather than merely of woundedness?

¡TABITA, LEVÁNTATE!

There is a story in the book of Hechos, in the Christian scriptures, about a woman named Tabita. She is considered a member of the early church and a discipula de Jesús. Because of her deep spiritual beliefs in the power of Christ, she clothed and cared for those in her community. You could say that Tabita, also known as Dorcas, was a chingona. She was a bold woman of healing and charitable acts.

Like her mentor, Jesús, Tabita transcended death. When she died, she was resurrected by Peter with the words: "Tabita, levántate." Tabitha, get up! Thus she was able to continue with her good acts and rich spiritual life. The name Tabita is Aramaic, a language that was originally spoken in Mesopotamia. It was the language that Jesus spoke. A short time before Peter's prayer raised Tabitha, Jesus himself had said the words "Talitha koum" (Little girl, get up!) to a little girl *he* was raising from the dead. (See Mark 5 and Acts 9 for these stories.)

The similarities between Tabitha and Talitha are not accidental; Jesus often used wordplay as an educational tool, like many rabbis of his time. Talitha is word for "child" in Aramaic, but in Hebrew it means "wounded lamb." Jesus's listeners, including Peter himself, would have understood this as a wordplay given that the region where Jesus grew up was multicultural and multilingual. Most of us feel like Tabita at times—like we are dead to the world, a child with no breath, a wounded lamb. Remember the legend of Popocatepetl and Iztaccíhuatl? We may not like to admit it, but sometimes we long to be carried.

A few years ago, I restarted the search for my biological father. I have started and stopped this process more times than I'd like to admit. Finally, I thought, I had built up enough courage to reach out and take the steps to find my father, who I haven't seen since I was three years old. But as soon as the pandemic hit and we were all sheltering in place, I let the coronavirus become the reason I couldn't go looking. "I can't go looking for him *now*; all I'll find is COVID!" I said to friends. Joking around is what I do when something is uncomfortable and hard to admit.

The truth, however, is that what stopped my search was not fear of the virus but fear of what wouldn't be there if I finally found him. Searching for something like love and then not finding it is more painful than not searching at all. Love could not possibly be there at the end of my search; at least that's what I told myself. I have held onto that narrative for longer than I can recall.

It was too scary to find out what the unknown part of me was made of. I was afraid I might learn that a part of my identity was actually irredeemable, unlovable. Over the years, through intention and therapy and the slow work of healing, I had forgiven this man for his abandonment. Yet a part of me ceased flourishing when he left. A part of me has stayed overwhelmed by the grief of his departure. It's almost like, long ago, a part of me died.

The part of me that stopped growing wanted to be loved. That part of me longed to resume a father-daughter journey again. But just as soon as I would feel that longing, my body would remember. It is not possible to be nurtured and protected, I'd tell myself. It is not possible to receive that type of love.

As an adult, I can understand that, for whatever reason, my biological father could not show up for me. Logically I know now that he simply could not love me the way I needed to be loved. My adult brain can all too easily detach and analyze in this methodical way. But the sense of abandonment? The memory of that feeling of being abandoned has lived on, stuck within my body. At times it has made me feel like a wounded lamb. A little child.

The seven-year-old me couldn't reason herself out of this rejection. She lived deserted, continually mourning the loss of her father.

WOUNDED LAMB, LITTLE CHILD

With the help of a therapist, I dove deeper into why my whole psyche sometimes felt like a seven-year-old girl who needs her father rather than like an adult woman. And I realized the extent of a deeper wound. It was at age seven that I first experienced sexual abuse at the hands of an older cousin. The abuse went on for a few months. The metaphysical wound of this abuse affected me deeply, and my sense of confidence and self-worth plummeted.

There was no other time in life when I longed so much for the protection of a father. In fact, it was after this event when I first asked the adults in my life to look for my dad. I was scared to tell them what had actually happened to me, but I hoped that my father's presence might somehow restore my innocence.

As an adult in therapy I recognized, rationally, that the psychological impact of this type of injury often includes blaming oneself. Yet when the realization of my abuse came crashing down on me, I considered never returning to my therapist's office. Even though I knew better, I felt like I was responsible for what happened to me. I wanted to escape myself. I wanted to undermine myself because the pain of the memory and abuse and abandonment was, at times, so much to bear.

For years, I dealt with this sexual trauma in a similar way as those who are unaware of the effects of colonization do: we harm ourselves. I engaged in violence against my own body, my own spirit. I did this by neglecting myself, abandoning myself in the same way I felt my father abandoned me. I didn't listen to my own emotional needs. I hid behind pride by not allowing others, friends or lovers alike, to get close. I sought comfort in objectifying and being objectified by men. It offered some relief from the sexual oppression I had experienced.

In fact, my sexual trauma, and the way it affected me afterward, is a bit like the history of settler colonialism and its continuing effects today. Settler colonialism is colonialism that replaces Indigenous populations with settlers, who set up their own society, government, and systems. On this continent, settler colonialism began centuries ago, but most scholars define settler colonialism as a structure rather than a single event during a single epoch. As writer Scott Morgensen says, settler colonialism is "an ongoing and ever-changing structure that defines everything in settler states."

The trauma of sexual abuse, and the trauma of colonialism, often occurs in a particular moment, at a specific time. The offense happens, and the immediate trauma is great. But the trauma isn't once-and-done. The memory and the legacy—of both abuse and settler colonialism—live on. Dehumanization, as a process, can have effects on all aspects of one's identity—on the whole structure, the very foundation, of your being. Once you've been dehumanized, it becomes a bit easier to dehumanize yourself and others.

As a young adult, I was deep in the process of exploiting and objectifying myself because of the way this sexual knowledge was impressed upon me as a child. Armed with red lipstick and a miniskirt, in my early twenties, I danced with complete strangers and looked for sexual conquests. During those years I thought that my free approach to sexuality was my way to be subversive, to revolt against the toxic empire of masculinity within my body. I enjoyed being indecente, embodying sexual aggression.

But these sexual adventures became a way for me to hide from the little child within, the wounded lamb. I wasn't allowing my true self to come forward. Those encounters also were not enough; I needed more of the excitement each time, to feel the rush once more. The rush of sexual conquest helped to cloud the "why?" plaguing my mind; it helped to quiet my questions.

It can be terrifying to look inward when you have silenced your own voice for so long. Thankfully, it came back. Over time, through therapy and with the help of friends, I finally was able to reconcile with the part of me that was scared, confused, and unloved—the little girl inside who had abandoned herself over and over again. I had quelled her for too long.

As long as we live in disharmony with ourselves, we keep the scar tissue from forming. But when we name our wounds—from colonialism to sexual abuse to a sense of abandonment to whatever the wound may be—we stop hiding from ourselves. We become more visible to ourselves and to others.

Because here's the thing: scars can connect us to both ourselves and to others. "We are all wounded, but we can connect through the wound that's alienated us from others," writes Gloria Anzaldúa. "The scar can become a bridge linking people split apart."

THE SACRED PRACTICE OF LIVING IN HARMONY, JOY, AND PEACE

Sometimes I still downplay my own unresolved issues with the father I have since found but to whom I have not spoken. "Daddy issues: so cliché, so played out," I hear myself say. It's an unsuccessful attempt to minimize my pain. Rather than trying to subvert this pain, I am trying to reclaim it.

We do not stand alone in the dark recesses of our hearts; Creator stands with us. If the divine exists, it does so in all aspects of life. I believe Diosito exists all around us, in all the violent masculinity, the daddy issues, the abandonment, and the self-inflicted violence. We remain mijas of the divine. God existed in the void and nothingness, in the wounded child and the unnecessary shame. The Great Spirit is there. Through all of it, a spiritual force is standing there with me in the darkness, on the precipice of finding harmony with myself once again, of being brought back to life, toward healing.

A subversive dignity is beginning to emerge for me. I think back to the words of the padres of my childhood churches, who often quoted Luke 12:2: "Nothing is covered up that will not be revealed, or hidden that will not be known."

Nothing is covered that will not be revealed. Nothing is hidden than will not be known. Telling this to the seven-year-old me offers her peace and comfort. My inner child is no longer silenced and ignored. In fact, she has become my teacher. She carries the wisdom of my ancestors, who both inflicted and received so much psychic pain.

My seven-year-old self knows something about betrayal— something I could only admit when I let down the walls I erected against myself. Listening to my seven-year-old self has allowed me to find harmony and begin trusting myself again. She reminds me that the kingdom of the divine belongs to her (Mark 10:14). The scar has become a bridge linking me back to her.

Being responsive to the spiritual realm has allowed me to understand who I really am, and all of who I am makes me mija of the divine. Ultimately, the traumas happened *to* me; they are not me. The hiding from myself, the pain of the spiritual wound, the continued wounding of myself—through it all, I know now that the divine stands with me. I am able to find joy and peace by accepting the love and protection of a divine Father, the masculine elder, who is also a part of the divine. God loves that seven-year-old me, and God wants to bring her back from the dead. Levántate!

Violence is the result of toxic ideologies and empires. Violence is one of the lingering effects of colonization on the colonized. It is freeing to realize that it wasn't my own inability to protect myself as a child or the silence that I carried for so long that allowed violence to exist. As we heal from violence, it's comforting to know that so many people are working to create a safer and more loving world. Together we create a matrix of scars—patterns of healing strong enough to hold up renewed structures in our society. Our scars, our cicatrizes, build a bridge from the flesh to the spiritual, to our mindbodyspirit connection, and to community.

This brings me hope. Together we can imagine a world where we think differently, where we speak up and question deeply. We can replace paradigms of war with a paradigm of peace with ourselves. We can imagine a world without violence. We can imagine a world where we sit with the trauma we carry in our bodies and let it teach us. We can be in community with others and tell each other about our cicatrizes. Vulnerability is that wisdom that allows us to mend and care for ourselves. The cicatrizes do not have to alienate us from each other or from the divine. Cicatrizes teach us that both woundedness and healing are a part of who we are. Scars can teach us how to live in harmony, joy, and peace.

8

OUR CHINGONA ANCESTRY

Build a Bridge to Healing and Justice

I'm sixty-two and I feel like I'm not even halfway to being the chingona I want to be.

—SANDRA CISNEROS

When I set out to write this book, I had just come out of a cycle of spiritual deaths and rebirths. My spirit had been crushed by the weight of expectations, both my own and those forced upon me. I had to die to the images of myself that my family, community, and society had ready for me.

As brown women the world often tries to conquer, we cannot afford to live out other people's expectations. We cannot afford to be afraid of who we have become. The imaginative and free-ing work of healing ourselves and helping our communities fight for justice demands we summon the courage and strength needed to become chingonas. "It takes a long time for women to feel it's all right to be chingona. To aspire to be a chingona!" writes novelist Sandra Cisneros. "You are saying, 'This is my camino, this is my path and I'm gonna follow it, regardless of what culture says.' I don't think the church likes chingonas. I don't think the state likes chingonas! And fathers definitely do not like chingonas."

One reason I chose to study education was because I did not believe I was creative enough to study literature. What fueled my fire, however, were the writers: poets and artists I eventually encountered in my educational path. Sandra Cisneros, Jimmy Santiago Baca, Rudolfo Anaya, Cherríe Moraga—these writers opened a world for me. If I had been denied the opportunity to learn from them early in my life, I thought, what *else* have I not learned? What else do I not know about me and mi gente? So I decided to study learning itself. The people I list here happen to be Chicano artists, but in all cultures we have artists, dancers, poets, playwrights, and novelists.

Those the rest of the world has tried to conquer are creative. We create in ourselves the life we want, and we create the world we want around us too. Being a chingona is a nepantla state: in-between, almost but not there yet. It is an active practice of *being*. Of creating. This is why chingonas become a bridge of hope to future generations, breaking oppressive cycles and reclaiming hope in the process as we age. As we have seen in this book, the work of personal healing and social justice is creative, spiritually grounding, and system-defying work. Y entre mas vieja mas chingona.

I am here to tell you that you are the dreams of many chingonas of the past: warrior-queen ancestors who embodied survivance. Our chingona ancestors did more than survive; they practiced survivance. They birthed flourishing visions onto the future: you and me. Our antepasados—all those chingona ancestors who came before us—birthed generations of healers and helpers. I am not just speaking metaphorically here. I really do believe that when we work for healing and justice in ourselves and our communities, we are operating from deep ancestral roots of wisdom within us. Like firmly rooted trees of life, we have branches and shade to cover a wide ground. We outstretch our limbs to embrace it all: lo feo y lo bonito. Our chingona ancestors have a lot of wisdom to teach us about growth and creativity and healing and justice.

Some chingonas from the past get plenty of recognition. There are famous chingonas like Joan Baez, whose singing voice became the background music of the 1960s protest movements and who has been recognized for her musical resistance. As a child, Sylvia Mendez became well known for being expected to go to a segregated school in California but who instead, alongside her parents, fought and won the first US case in favor of desegregation so Mexican children like herself could go to school with white children. More recently, Raffi Freedman-Gurspan made history by becoming the first openly transgender person to become a White House staffperson. These chingonas are some of the well-recognized workers for healing and justice.

Workers of healing and justice come in various forms. Some, like the ones I mention above, change and influence laws. Others influence our spirits and hearts with their words. Cherríe Moraga first taught me that "sometimes a breakdown can be the beginning of a kind of breakthrough, a way of living in advance through a trauma that prepares you for a future of radical transformation." She and other chingona writers like Ana Castillo dare to not be tamed. They use their words to weave the personal and the political. Owning your inner chingona is both personal and political.

Contemporary capitalism depends on generational cycles of apathy and violence for its survival. But many freedom fighters have intervened in these oppressive systems, showing us paths not of least resistance but of liberation and justice. These liberatory ancestors fought for the rights of farmworkers to have humane working conditions, including a living wage, breaks to rest, and manageable shifts. Seasoned chingonas like Dolores Huerta and Maria Moreno, farmworkers and labor organizers whose work has honored the hard work of their communities, dared to imagine living in a new type of system and dared to intervene in order to actualize those ideas. I think of the many contemporary hotel workers across the United States who are unionizing and fighting for higher pay and safe working environments free of mistreatment. They are chingona ancestors, too—creating change in their own backyards and their places of work.

Some of the chingonas I have learned from were radical, revolutionary ancestors: antepasados who worked hard to keep love, hope, and our imaginations alive. I draw so much hope and love from these chingonas. And then there are my literal chingona ancestors, my own tias and abuelas. These women simply demonstrated survivance: resistance to all kinds of domination in the workplace and at home. They were the first chingonas to teach me that change is possible and who taught me how to practice hope when all seemed hopeless.

So many chingonas' names are lost to history. In fact, most of the chingona ancestors who propel us into the future are forgotten and unsung. Like them, some of us might never be recognized beyond our own families, group of friends, or coconspirators. Rather than cause for concern, however, this lack of attention to our work gives us the freedom to imagine even more wildly and loudly the type of future systems we want.

What if *we* could become that type of ancestor for future generations? What would it look like for you to situate yourself alongside liberatory ancestors? In what ways could you intervene for future generations? What will be your chingona legacy?

CHINGONA LEGACY

If you've read this far, you know I am the product of a painful legacy. I have been deeply hurt, in various personal and sociohistorical ways. My heart, mind, and body have needed tending and mending. I have had to learn to speak up for myself and to break generational cycles of abuse, untreated mental illness, and addiction. But no matter what legacy we've been handed, we can choose to heal ourselves and to build and repair that bridge to hope and love. I had erroneously believed that owning my inner chingona was a lonely, isolated task. But I have stepped back to see my wider and longer lineage and legacy. Creating and believing in an imagined future and practicing hope is something my ancestors taught me.

The work toward social regeneration feels unattainable at times. How can we truly transform the world when we have so much to get through individually, within ourselves? Will our current collective efforts make any difference to future generations? Where has subverting the system taken us? Isn't it better to just do as we are told, to believe that the systems we have created are just fine? That those systems are there for a reason? That the way we've set up the world is the best we could do?

But our conditioning limits our understanding of the choices we have, and it limits the creativity we can exert. It maintains the status quo. The key to social change via healing is knowing that we are socialized to choose the path of least resistance—*and* that other paths exist. Once you know how deeply we are all conditioned, you can avoid reproducing the past, both in your own healing and with those around you. You can learn from the many chingonas who did not choose the path of least resistance and instead chose paths of healing and justice.

Capitalism, class systems, and other oppressive structures are maintained when we choose paths of least resistance. Taking the path of least resistance is easy—to give in to the systems around us and to believe in the unjust laws and generational cycles that promise to safeguard our children and whatever material goods we have accumulated. It's easy to get carried along by the rivers of dead beliefs and values, to sit in our comfortable floats of organized religion or economic privilege or a politician's promises. But when the processes we have created no longer work, we must change.

Breaking the cycle of injustice is incredibly hard work. Definitions of "justice" privilege the wealthy because, historically, that is who has defined it: those in positions of power, those who have colonized the other. Our country's current ways of doing things are fueled by old regimes and ideologies: colonization and conquest and control. Those ideologies come disguised in feelings of protection and safety and comfort. Not reproducing this world but regenerating it means leaving behind that sense of safety and comfort. It means reimagining ourselves and what could be. It means actually reclaiming, for ourselves, what it means to be a divine and cosmic community and how we want to treat each other and create a sustainable world.

When the needle points to the path of least resistance, we must reimagine ourselves and our systems. We must readjust the compass toward hope, love, and change. What if we could make borders, hierarchies, othering, and exclusion things of the past? What if we could parent as we wish our parents could have parented us? Could we see the future as one of love and joy, not fear, and let that vision dictate how we relate to one another? Could we join the long ancestral line of chingonas who look at the path of least resistance and then choose another camino?

PRACTICING HOPE AND LOVE

Being a chingona means transforming the anger we have about the system and those stuck in the status quo. Learning our own history helps in this process. Rather than allowing history to dictate who the losers are, we can question why we have to operate in a system dependent on winners and losers. Yes, our histories are filled with colonization, patriarchy, violence, and superiority complexes, and the anger that results when we realize the extent to which this is true can be overwhelming. In those times, we need to place ourselves in safe containers so that we do not replicate harm by projecting it onto others. Even amid that anger, we must not lose trust in the possibility for change. It is hard to shift from anger to possibility, but we can focus on how other chingonas have bridged to hope.

Practicing hope is hard. Every time a company or a government or an educational system prioritizes greed and privilege over human lives, we can get disillusioned. But chingonas can see beyond reality and into the code that lies beneath it. Seeing patterns across the system is what helped me to see beyond the seams, to bridge to hope and imagine possibilities. It is also something I now consider a gift. There is something special about being able to see the code, much like Neo from *The Matrix* franchise did when he was given the option of seeing reality. Seeing the simulation made me angrier than seeing the reality, but being aware of both gave me perspective to question and imagine change.

I don't take for granted the fact that I narrowly escaped the fate of many others around me. Escaping generational cycles of abuse and not going to jail, I avoided feeling disempowered and becoming a victim of a merciless system. But seeing how easily I could have ended up trapped in an unforgiving and controlling system has made me grateful. Changing that system has become my purpose.

I would be lying if I didn't acknowledge that I sometimes forget my actual purpose in challenging and reimagining the status quo. As we challenge systems, chingonas sometimes find ourselves sucked into the grind. We become complicit in a colonial mentality. This is the uncomfortable reality: existing within a predesigned system, we sometimes reflect that system even in our critique of it. Being a chingona means accepting this reality, that we have to somehow survive within the status quo while also naming the seams and subverting the whole toxic setup.

I come back to questioning and protesting the status quo again and again. I cannot let myself forget the manufactured borders that limit us, and I need to remain cognizant that the futures we imagine for ourselves are limited by what is rehearsed to us in society. Existing in multiple intersectional identities throughout my life has helped me notice the seams of the system, the way different systems oppress us based on our ethnicity, education, and income. Ultimately, my own intersecting identities help me translate oppression and privilege for others who cannot see it. Chingonas are cultural workers who translate for others, and as a result we help others reimagine legacy.

ANCESTRAL WISDOM AS SPIRITUAL ACTIVISM

Our bodies channel both our ancestors' trauma and their survivance. Our bodies channel the pain and suffering but also the resilience and growth. I am not only talking about genes but also how living with stress and in survival mode alter our bodies. Due to the trauma of colonization, my ancestors carried incredible stories of adaptation and survival in the harshest of circumstances.

My experiences living in emotional, physical, and spiritual borderlands point to an interconnectedness in us all. This lesson— that we are all interconnected—does not feel accidental; it is metaphysical, a remembering of linear and nonlinear realities operating all at once. And so I dream of a world with communal reciprocity and mutuality. Where we revere children for their proximity to this remembering: "How easy it is for children to trust and love wholeheartedly." We know in our bones that we are each other's otro yo—"my other me." In a poem called "Pensamiento Serpentino," Chicano playwright Luis Valdez draws on the Mayan virtue known as "In Lak'ech," or "you are the other me." This is an idea that shows up in many cultures around the world. South African writer Mungi Ngomane, the granddaughter of Desmond Tutu, describes the concept of ubuntu: I am because you are. Seeing from each other's perspective helps us tend to each other and respect our terrestrial home. Indigenous cultures in the United States and Canada value the concept of "we are all related."

When I fall short of this remembering, I can count on others to remind me. This is what chingonas must do: we must find ways to remind each other of all that we are creating. Stepping into our chingona ancestry means understanding our interconnectedness with each other, with our ancestors, and with generations to come. Gathering with each other in community fortifies this understanding.

Ancestral wisdom continues to remind me daily of this interconnectedness. My heart breaks for those stuck in the controlling mechanisms of our society: generational cycles of addiction, unjust laws, impunity of the wealthy, kids in cages, a disproportionate number of Black and brown men and women in jail, homelessness, intimate partner violence, the wealthy getting wealthier, and the greed of corporations destroying our planet, which is our collective home. Before I embraced my inner chingona, I couldn't accept these realities, and they used to take me down a dark hole of despair. Just thinking about all the ways that humans have screwed up in the world made me so upset that I almost convinced myself I could not do anything about it, that it was a futile endeavor altogether to try to change. Before I experienced the slow unfolding of healing in my own mind and body, the injustices I saw everywhere used to trigger such profound anxiety that I would be unable to function for days.

But in those moments, we can recall the power of change we have seen in our chingona ancestors: to imagine different possibilities, and then fight for justice in small and big ways. Our ancestors remind us daily that we can unlearn helplessness and learn to hold the tension of what is and what could be. In each other, we find what Angela Davis calls "reservoirs of hope and activism." While we may not see true justice achieved in our lifetimes, within our communities we find what we need.

The young adults I mentor often ask me what they should do in terms of choosing their majors and then their careers. In those moments, I love to step back and help them reframe the question. I like to do this both because they will have to reconfigure the questions for themselves in the future and learn to ask the deeper questions, and also because stepping into chingona ancestry means becoming the type of mentor I wish I once had. So I often tell the younger "me's" that what we *do* doesn't matter so much as *why* and *how* we do it. What is the legacy you want to leave behind? I ask them. What do you ground yourself in? Because what you view as the purpose of your existence defines how you show up in the world. Sometimes it's religious or spiritual values that ground the young adults with whom I work; sometimes it's an ethic of collective love. Other times it boils down to money and accumulation of nice objects—what the world wants them to believe is true success. There are as many things to do for a living as there are people, but what we ground ourselves in matters. We cannot know that we are grounded in something until we ask why we do what we do and how we are showing up for ourselves and others. Awareness of and belief in ourselves—that we are worth the fight—helps us move together toward repair and change. I believe that our collective work toward loving one another is why we are here. We are meant to fully experience and live every moment with others. My healing also means chasing freedom and transformative justice in community with others.

My work includes deepening in ancestral wisdom what Gloria Anzaldúa calls "spiritual activism." We are here to reimagine and take pleasure in the world we create together. There are different ways to do this work, and sharing our ancestral wisdom is a part of it.

Due to the personal trauma and pain I experienced as a kid and as an adult, I have had to become the type of ancestor I wanted and needed. I've always been sensitive to the spiritual realm, what Zaida Maldonado Pérez calls a "wild child of the spirit": a strong-willed child of the divine. My own lived experiences in personal healing include my journey with my curandero, Jesus. I view Jesus as my healer of mental, emotional, physical, and spiritual illnesses. As I reimagine faith, I see the possibility that faith can coexist with embodied compassion.

For a long time, being fueled by coraje, I developed an oppositional attitude toward anyone in power. But as I grew in recognizing my own power, privilege, and complicit colonial mentality, this was hard to reconcile. I learned to balance my coraje—my courage and anger—with compassion for others feeling the same type of exclusion, oppression, and disposability. I have begun creating sacred mujer spaces, in my home and with others, where we can show up to remind ourselves of our ancestral wisdom and strength. We talk about therapy, faith, and justice, as well as topics that are sometimes thought to be contradictory. We hold nepantla space. We exist together in our marginality and in our power. For chingonas who have felt the spirit of oppression within our families, these alternative faith spaces remind us that we can harness our creativity and legacy.

Our chingona legacy is about reclaiming our spiritual and emotional healing journey. It is about continuing the resistance and transformational work of our antepasados. This type of generational wealth offers hope and peace to future generations. As I was nurtured and built up by other chingonas who understood and did not misuse their power, I learned to recognize the power within me and the need to speak up. This change within me also encouraged those around me. With compassion and with power, I learned to speak up for myself, to name the wounds, and to find healing in community with others who had similar experiences. As I healed and owned my inner chingona, I helped others to name and heal too.

This is my chingona legacy: the leveraging of power in a redemptive way. I hold this ancestral remembering so that I use my power differently. The pain of being excluded and viewed as disposable by society taught me that society is just a representation of our fractured selves. Our chingona legacy is about awakening to the fractures within ourselves and each other in order to heal and create a more just world. Change begins with ourselves.

Whether you are aware of it yet or not, you are not alone in your struggle. You never have been. When the world tries to conquer brown women, we surround each other with support. When the world screams fear and hate, chingonas step up and yell back love and joy.

ACKNOWLEDGMENTS

"At some point, on our way to a new consciousness, we will have to leave the opposite bank, the split between the two mortal combatants somehow healed so that we are on both shores at once and, at once, see through serpent and eagle eyes."

—Gloria Anzaldua

I want to thank the chingon/as that made writing this book possible: Jason "Prop" Petty, Valerie Weaver-Zercher, Carlos Martinez, Trinity McFadden, and Maria "Mer" Young. Your support and encouragement made it so I could not resist writing and creating. Jason—mi amor y compañero del alma. Que corny! Thank you for holding down the home front while I escaped to write and then to rest from writing. This book took so much physical, emotional, and spiritual labor, and without your support I would not have shared my brown girl story. Valerie, I am so indebted to you for believing in my work and voice. Your writing feedback and our synergy made me go deeper into creative and spiritual memories and ideas. I will let you know when I'm ready for "mija spirituality." Carlos—mi terapista turned friend and mentor. Gracias por tu apoyo. You stepped up in a time I really needed to believe this book was possible. Even if it took an unexpected (totally expected) turn.

Trinity—the agent that made book magic happen. So grateful for your advice, advocacy, and demystifying the process. Meeerrrrr! Your art on my cover is the cherry on top; it makes it all come together perfectly. Gracias por tu vision, amiga.

Mi Luna y Soul, the chingonitas who made me a mother: I've learned so much from you, and my only wish is that I become the mother you need. Thank you for your im/patience during the process; it made me more focused and determined to complete the book.

Mil gracias to the women who held and helped me grow through some difficult times. Too many to list, and for that I am so grateful. My heart is so full. You are why I can see through serpent and eagle eyes. Our communal care inspired this book.

Dedico este libro a mi familia. Mi papa, Abraham. Mi mama, Elsa. Por todos sus sacrificios y amor. A mi hermana y hermano, Lizeth y Jose. Por su amistad y por aguantar a una segunda madre.

NOTES

CHAPTER 1

3   *"Like Brown, I am committed to"*: Adrienne Maree Brown, "This Is the Moment for Visionary Narratives," *Immerse*, December 14, 2016, https://immerse.news/this-is-the-moment-for-visionary-narratives-7db0d9797ec1#.mq3n0gdmk.

4   *"The first people referred to as"*: "Hijas de la Chingada! Este Es El Origen de la Palabra 'Chingar,'" Milenio, January 8, 2019, https://www.milenio.com/cultura/chingar-origen-y-significado-de-la-palabra.

7   *"It is a limited space, a space where"*: Gloria Anzaldúa, *Borderlands/La Frontera* (San Francisco: Aunt Lute Books, 1987), 276.

7   *"As she writes, I was"*: AnaLouise Keating, "From Borderlands and New Mestizas to Nepantla and Nepantleras: Anzaldúan Theories for Social Change," *Human Architecture: Journal of the Sociology of Self-Knowledge* 4, no. 3 (2006): 5–16.

7   *"I wanted to use what"*: Dolores Delgado Bernal, "Using a Chicana Feminist Epistemology in Educational Research," *Harvard Educational Review* 68, no. 4 (1998): 555–83.

7   *"I knew I would not find"*: For more on this idea of intuition as a guide, see Clarissa Pinkola Estes and Caroline Myss, *Intuition and the Mystical Life: Caroline Myss and Clarissa Pinkola Estes Bring Women's Wisdom to Light* (Louisville, CO: Sounds True, 2009).

8   *"Finding conocimiento—a wisdom"*: See Anzaldúa, *Borderlands*; and Anzaldúa, "Now Let Us Shift . . . the Path of Conocimiento . . . Inner Work, Public Acts," in *This Bridge We Call Home: Radical Visions for Transformation*, ed. Gloria Anzaldúa and AnaLouise Keating (New York: Routledge, 2002), 540–78.

10 *"I was trying to find a"*: Carrie Hansen, "How Melina Duarte Modernized the Word Chingona and How Sandra Cisneros Inspires Latinas," Vizaca, January 13, 2021, https://www.vizaca.com/chingona-meaning/.

11 *"What truly defines us as chingonas"* Angela Aguirre, "How I Define My Chingona Fire," *HuffPost*, January 24, 2017, https://www.huffpost.com/entry/how-i-define-my-chingona-fire_b_5887de69e4b0a53ed60c6a35.

12 *"This book includes glimpses of"*: See Daniel G. Solorzano and Tara J. Yosso, "Critical Race Methodology: Counter-Storytelling as an Analytical Framework for Education Research," *Qualitative Inquiry* 8, no. 1 (2002): 23–44, https://journals.sagepub.com/doi/abs/10.1177/107780040200800103.

18 ***"What if we approached our"***: Jennifer Guerra Aldana et al., "Ancestral Wisdom: Storytelling," from *Café with Comadres Podcast*, October 20, 2021, https://anchor.fm/cafewithcomadres /episodes/Ancestral-Wisdom-Communing-With-Our-Ancestors -e17f5np.

CHAPTER 2

27 ***"Some writers, including Elena Avila"***: Elena Avila, *Woman Who Glows in the Dark: A Curandera Reveals Traditional Aztec Secrets of Physical and Spiritual Health* (New York: TarcherPerigree, 2000).

27 ***"They understand the historical and"***: Sara Alicia Ramirez, "Subjects of Trauma: The Decolonial Tactics of Self-Making and Self-Healing by Queer Xicana Feminist Teatristas" (PhD diss., University of California, Berkeley, 2016), https://eschol arship.org/content/qt6wc1k0s9/qt6wc1k0s9_noSplash_2f58ec b0a6c32c71095f3eb9ae16a72b.pdf?t=omfvzh.

CHAPTER 3

72 ***"I thought this reunion would offer"***: Gustavo Arellano, "Prop 187 Timeline: The Rise and Fall of California's Anti-Immigrant Law," *Los Angeles Times*, October 29, 2019, https://www.latimes. com/california/story/2019-10-06/proposition-187-timeline.

CHAPTER 4

75   *"According to a recent news article":* James Pasley and Angela Wang, "The 50 Most Miserable Cities in America, Based on Census Data," *Business Insider,* September 28, 2019, https://www.businessinsider.com/most-miserable-cities-in-the-united-states-based-on-data-2019-9#10-huntington-park-california-41.

87   *"A story can be used to otherize or":* Chimimanda Ngozi Adichie, "The Danger of a Single Story," July 2009, https://www.ted.com/talks/chimamanda_ngozi_adichie_the_danger_of_a_single_story?language=en.

88   *"We will only be free when, as":* Aurora Levins Morales, *Medicine Stories: Essays for Radicals* (Durham, NC: Duke University Press, 2019), 49.

99   *"But it's also about* **survivance***":* "Decolonizing the Archive: Indigenous People and Survivance," Early Caribbean Digital Archive, Northeastern University, accessed December 13, 2021, https://ecda.northeastern.edu/home/about/decolonizing-the-archive/decolonizing-the-archive-indigenous-people-and-survivance/.

CHAPTER 5

102   *"Confronted with the colonial order":* Frantz Fanon, *The Wretched of the Earth* (New York: Grove Press, 1963), 16.

113 *"In these educational systems"*: Bettina L. Love, *We Want to Do More Than Survive: Abolitionist Teaching and the Pursuit of Educational Freedom* (Boston: Beacon Press, 2019), 27.

115 *"The pulse of what bell hooks calls"*: Interview with bell hooks, "Cultural Criticism and Transformation," Media Education Foundation, transcript accessed November 15, 2021, https://www.mediaed.org/transcripts/Bell-Hooks-Transcript.pdf.

118 *"Nepantla es tierra desconocida"*: Gloria Anzaldúa, in *This Bridge Called Home: Radical Visions for Transformation*, ed. Anzaldúa and AnaLouise Keating (New York: Routledge, 2002), 1.

119 *"Living means facing continuous"*: https://iep.utm.edu/aztec /#SH2b.

119 *"For Aztecs, discernment grows"*: Miguel Leon-Portilla, *Aztec Thought and Culture: A Study of the Ancient Nahuatl Mind*, trans. J. Davis (Norman: University of Oklahoma Press, 1963).

121 *"Latinas make up only about"*: Anne-Marie Nuñez and Elizabeth Murakami-Ramalho, "The Demograhic Dividend," American Association of University Professors, January–February 2012, https://www.aaup.org/article/demographic-dividend# .Yae8OfHMI-Q.

128 *"We miss the fact that somewhere"*: See Alice Walker, *We Are the Ones We Have Been Waiting For: Inner Light in a Time of Darkness* (New York: The New Press, 2006).

CHAPTER 7

162 *"In fact, my sexual trauma":* Nelson Maldonado-Torres, "Outline of Ten Theses on Coloniality and Decoloniality," Frantz Fanon Foundation and website of the Caribbean Studies Association, October 26, 2016, http://fondation-frantzfanon .com/outline-of-ten-theses-on-coloniality-and-decoloniality/.

162 *"As writer Scott Morgensen says":* Scott Lauria Morgensen, *Spaces between Us: Queer Settler Colonialism and Indigenous Decolonization* (Minneapolis: University of Minnesota Press, 2011), 2.

164 *"We are all wounded":* Gloria Anzaldúa, *Light in the Dark/Luz en lo Oscuro: Rewriting Identity, Spirituality, Reality* (Durham, NC: Duke University Press, 2015), 21.

CHAPTER 8

170 *"You are saying, 'This":* Sandra Cisneros, *The Latino List,* directed by Timothy Greenfield-Sanders, HBO, aired September 29, 2011.

172 *"Cherríe Moraga first taught me":* Cherríe Moraga, Gloria Anzaldúa, and Toni Cade Bambara, *This Bridge Called My Back: Writings by Radical Women of Color* (Albany, NY: State University of New York Press, 1981).

180 ***"Seeing from each other's":*** See Luis Valdez, "Pensamiento Serpentino," El Teatro Campesino, 1973 (a portion of this poem, known as "In Lak'ech," was unconstitutionally outlawed in public schools in Tucson, Arizona); Mungi Ngomane, *Everyday Ubuntu: Living Better Together, the African Way* (New York: Harper Design, 2020); and Patty Krawec, *Becoming Kin: An Indigenous Call to Unforgetting the Past and Reimagining Our Future* (Minneapolis: Broadleaf Books, 2022).

181 ***"Our ancestors remind us":*** Angela Davis, *Freedom Is a Constant Struggle: Ferguson, Palestine, and the Foundations of a Movement* (New York: Haymarket Books, 2016).

183 ***"My work includes deepening":*** For more unpacking of this concept, see Elisa Facio and Irene Lara, eds., *Fleshing the Spirit: Spirituality and Activism in Chicana, Latina, and Indigenous Women's Lives* (Tucson: Arizona University Press, 2014).

183 ***"I've always been sensitive":*** Loida I. Martell, Zaida Maldonado Pérez, and Elizabeth Conde-Frazier, *Latina Evangélicas: A Theological Survey from the Margins* (Seattle: Cascade Books, 2013).